To Lois
Love, Jayson

The Heart Remembers

A MEMOIR OF GROWTH THROUGH GRIEF

JAYSON WOODWARD

Disclaimer:
Every effort has been made to ensure this book is as accurate and complete as possible. However, there may be mistakes both typographical and in content. Therefore, this book should be used as a general guide and not and the ultimate source of information contained herein. The author and publisher shall not be liable or responsible to any person or entity with respect to any loss or damage caused or alleged to have been caused directly or indirectly by the information contained in this book.

Published by Jayson Woodward, produced by Indie Experts
www.AuthorityAuthors.com.au
QLD 4019, Australia

Cover design by Independent Ink
Edited by Deirdre Swanney
Internal design by Independent Ink
Typeset in 11/15.5 pt Goudy Old Style by Post Pre-press Group, Brisbane

ISBN: 978 0 578 57598 8

This book is dedicated to my beloved husband, Trey, who chose to share his life with me. His warm hospitality and Texas-sized heart gave so many the gift of learning to love the land. Without his gentle guidance, patience, and generosity, many would never have known the treasures to be found in the great outdoors. Here's to you, my partner, my teacher, my love, my friend!

Table of Contents

ACKNOWLEDGEMENTS

THERE ARE SO MANY PEOPLE who supported me throughout my personal journey and helped me in immeasurable ways to get this book written, that it is quite a task to thank them all.

First and foremost; my friend and business advisor, Bill Richmond, shared his extraordinary organizational skills to help me when I couldn't help myself. He brought caring and laughter to a very dark period in my life. I also thank my good friends Alec and Suze, who steadfastly stood by me, offering solace, encouragement, and a ready ear when I needed to talk. Michael's patient understanding, technical expertise, and unfailing friendship helped me to grow as a person as well as a writer. I also thank Phyllis for her reading of drafts of the book and her expert editing. Tony and Jan both shared their many talents in helping me to remain on the land. Marlene and her husband, Larry, traveled many long miles to support me with their friendship and encouragement. Fred and Robin helped so much during the darkest of days by selflessly offering their knowledge, support, caring and WORK! To so many others, who shall remain unnamed here, one and all, I thank you.

PRELUDE

MY HUSBAND, TREY, AND I lived an almost idyllic life. Living on his family's ranch, we avoided all the urban chaos of our time. Hard driven workaholics by nature, we both relished in the never-ending chores inherent in such a pastoral lifestyle. It was impossible to become bored; tired, yes, bored, no.

We had all the advantages of rural life, and very few of its disadvantages. Being a working ranch, we also had an income from ecotourism, or, as I liked to call it, helping the refugees from the city with all manner of their, delicately put, disturbances.

Visitors from their urban and suburban worlds would arrive at our remote ranch, frazzled, upset, unsure of themselves, and generally unable to align the vast and panoramic view with anything even moderately familiar to their model of existence. Due to the huge distances from any city, a journey to the ranch often meant the arrival of unsettled children, uncomfortable adults, and pitiful pets. We knew exactly how they felt, for when it was required that we visit any city, we were in the same condition. But on the ranch, it was our job to make things right.

With our best Texas manners, we welcomed visitors to the ranch seven days a week, and at any hour of the day or night. Working together we made a great team. Having been a teacher, it was my pleasure to relate the history of five generations of the ranch and show visitors the small Heritage museum that we built to house all the antiques and artifacts collected and saved by each generation. We often put on ranch dinners and bar-b-ques for our guests, without any charge. It was almost a mission to model a peaceful, harmonic, Texas way of life for our guests, if for no other reason than to give them a brief respite from the storms of urban life.

Also a working ranch, Trey divided his time between helping with our visitors and taking care of the cattle and the other chores of ranch life; fixing fences, fixing water systems and pumps, fixing roads, fixing pens . . . notice the emphasis on "fixing." Not a day goes by on a ranch without something needing to be repaired. He wasn't always good at it, but generally whatever was broken would work again, if only for a while. He was a genius at "re-purposing" all manner of things. He once sent me to the hardware store to buy a piece of hose he needed for some plumbing job. Unable to understand what kind of hose it was or what I should be asking the clerk for, he just said, "Here. Take this one and tell them you need one like this." I dutifully went to the hardware store with hose in hand. The astonished clerk looked quizzically at me and then said, "Ma'am, this is a radiator hose. You should go to the auto parts store."

And so life continued for some fourteen years; working hard, building the tourist business, building the cattle herd, loving each other and blessing the good fortune and the long wait that had finally brought us together. And then with no warning, Trey died.

Suddenly, inexplicably, as I sat next to his hospital bed, begging God or any super power to save his life, pleading, bartering, and wishing for it not to be so, my whole reality changed within eight hours.

Without change in our lives, existence would be a static bore. Think of it. No seasons. No development. No evolving. No learning. Change is what colors our lives with unexpected challenges. Change is the grist for human interaction with everything else that exists.

And yet, *sudden*, or *catastrophic* change can so damage us that we are left unable to cope with the most mundane daily tasks. Some species can tolerate no more than a few degrees of temperature change, dying when the limit is reached on one end of the continuum or the other. Human beings have a broader range of temperatures, sometimes existing in extreme cold, and somehow managing to stay cool in extreme heat. But we, too, have areas in our physical, mental and emotional beings that offer only a small degree of tolerance for change.

Most of us have within us the ability to inculcate changes into our developed framework of how the world *is*. Whatever we've designed to be our model of what is real is necessarily built to absorb, or deny, the experiences that continuously build that framework. This ability is primarily the talent that has led us to the top of the food chain. The way one perceives oneself before the change event can be quite painful to re-associate with new perceptions. Without being too clinical, the ability to change, however slowly, however painfully, is critical to all life.

It is helpful to have guideposts, signs, teachings and all manner of knowledge to inform us of how to proceed with inevitable change. It is helpful to know that someone has walked down a similar path before you. It is helpful to know that someone else has survived what feels like at the time a life-ending event.

It is in that spirit of sharing that this book is written.

1

THE BEGINNING

FOR TWO YEARS WE DIDN'T know anything was seriously wrong. As Trey's energy began to sag, I took on more and more of the ranch business. The first symptom we chalked up to "sore muscles." Trey went to the chiropractor for several sessions and the treatment didn't seem to help. Shoulder still sore, he went to a physician. "Bursitis," the doctor claimed, "happens when you age. Don't do so much physical work!"

"Well there's no chance of that!" Trey laughed. We continued going about our business, Trey resting his arm at times in a sling.

Then Trey's teeth became a problem. Yes, he'd had bad gums and teeth for years and we assumed it was catching up with him. After a round of dentists, and several weeks of internet research, we unknowingly picked the absolute worst choice we could have made and scheduled an appointment. The dentist *seemed* all right at first glance. His office was nice, he used sedation (I assumed he was an oral surgeon) and touted that as his most important skill. He also touted his experience with dental implants. Little did we know at the time that he'd had a few quick seminars on implants, had not kept up with ongoing best practices, and really, had little experience with them.

But trying to get the best care for Trey we could afford, we decided to have his natural teeth pulled (the recommendation of several previous dentists), dentures made, and four implants surgically embedded to hold the dentures in place. (Knowing Trey as I did, I could just visualize him getting fed up with trying to get used to regular dentures, taking them out in frustration and leaving them on a fence post somewhere!) It was an expensive proposition, $15,300.00 to be exact, but we put the expense on a credit card and scheduled the procedure.

We made several trips to Odessa to have Trey's mouth measured and impressions of his natural teeth made. The dentist then assured me that on the day of surgery, Trey would feel no pain, the procedure would take about an hour and a half, and he would then want something soft to eat afterwards. "Take him around the corner for a milkshake," the dentist said, "before you make the two hour drive back home. He'll probably sleep the whole way."

The day of the surgery arrived. It was a nightmare. Trey was called in to the procedure room about 2:00. Two hours went by. The nurse kept assuring me that everything was all right, but, "just taking a little longer than we expected." I sat in the waiting room watching other patients come in and, eventually, leave. By 6:00 I was through waiting. I walked down the narrow hall, looking for the treatment room that housed Trey. Finally, there he was. The dentist and assisting nurse looked up, startled, and said, "We're just about through here. Go back to the waiting room!" Trey was still unconscious, and the dentist again said it would only be a few more minutes, so I returned to the waiting room lobby.

Finally a nurse came to the lobby and instructed me to drive to the outside door where patients coming out of anesthesia were released. I left immediately and drove to the pick-up door. Trey couldn't walk. His face was swollen beyond recognition. Blood was all over his shirt. He had urinated in his jeans. He was barely conscious. Blood was coming out of his mouth. I caught a glimpse of the dentist as he stayed almost out of site in the doorway, showing only a bit of his profile. The nurse wheeled Trey to the car in a wheelchair and poured him into the passenger seat. She turned and started to close the car door. It was obvious she couldn't get back inside fast enough.

"Wait a minute!" I yelled, rising hysteria in my voice. "He looks terrible! What has happened?" I screamed at her.

"Well, he had a little trouble during the surgery, but he should be ok," she answered, with a very dubious look on her face. She looked as if she was ready to run.

"Aren't you even going to get a seat belt on him?" I asked.

"Oh, yes! That's right! I forgot, but we had better do that," she answered, looking embarrassed.

She strapped Trey in, slammed the car door and walked hurriedly away. I grabbed paper towels and held them to Trey's mouth. He was slowly starting to come around.

"Do you want some ice cream?" I inanely asked, not knowing what to do but remembering the dentist's earlier instructions. If I had not been on the verge of hysteria I would have jumped out of the car and run into the dentist's office to find out what had happened to get Trey in such awful condition. But more concerned about doing something for Trey in the moment, I drove around the block to an ice cream drive in.

At his mumbled request, I ordered a strawberry milkshake for him (his favorite flavor), thinking it would help revive him. When it arrived, I held it for him, but he couldn't use the straw. I spooned it into his mouth. He couldn't swallow. Blood poured out over the ice cream. The strawberry pink of the ice cream mixed with the bright red of blood pouring out of his mouth. He was trying to talk, but was out of his head . . . the words were jumbled and slurred and didn't make sense.

Petrified, I called my best friend in Midland and she insisted we come to her house for the night, so that we could give Trey the attention he needed. I drove the 40 miles or so to her house and dissolved into tears when she and her housekeeper came running out to the car to help support Trey and get him in to the house.

We got him undressed and into bed, then put ice packs around his entire face. My friend wasn't a nurse, but she had cared for parents and grandparents, and knew what to do. I stood there feeling stunned by the surgical outcome, betrayed by the dentist, and guilty because it had been at my insistence that Trey had opted for dentures in the first place.

With hindsight you gain perfect vision, and I can see now that, while the shoulder pain was a symptom of a fatal disease, the dental surgery tipped the scales and began the rapid deterioration of Trey's still unknown condition. But at that moment, it was just a poor outcome of dental surgery and an overworked and strained shoulder. As they say, "ignorance is bliss."

By midnight Trey's facial swelling had decreased quite a bit, and he was conscious and, almost, alert. At least he was hungry. We made mashed potatoes and gravy and spoon fed him, as his coordination was still uncontrollable. With each passing hour his condition improved, and by mid-morning we were loaded into the car and on our way back to the ranch.

It was late August, and as the end of the summer landscape flew by the windows of the car, I remember thinking about the season coming to an end. I believed the long days of Trey's illness, and worrying about illness, were ending, too. I thought the dental surgery would mark a turning point in his health and he could now begin to gain weight and re-gain energy. Sitting for the three hour drive home made me realize how tired I had become, and how stressed from the unrelenting, hot days of the summer and the never-ending chores to do on the ranch. I reasoned with myself that now my favorite time of year was about to begin. Fall always rejuvenates me, and I thought about all the fun things there were to do in association with this season, getting the ranch and the house ready for winter.

We'd rake the fruitless Mulberry tree leaves in the front yard and watch the horses come in to eat them for their favorite treat. We'd wrap all the pipes to keep them from freezing, and winterize the windows of the house to try and stop the leaks of cold air from settling into the house.

I love to cook and to bake, and fall is the perfect time. The oven keeps the house warm, and all the goodies would put weight back on Trey. I would, I daydreamed, be able to spend more time doing household chores, and less time playing cowgirl.

Sure, the surgery had been hard on Trey. People get sick, and sometimes things get medically scary, but it always turns out okay, just like this was turning out to be all right. Trey was a bit uncomfortable, but almost back to his old self again, complaining that it was too cold in the car, and that I was driving too slowly. I felt confident that this was the last hurdle to Trey's regained health, and I began to feel myself relax. Things were getting back to normal.

2

A SLOW DESCENT

As THE DENTIST HAD ORDERED, Trey stayed in bed for a couple of days. After that he got up for short periods, careful not to lift anything weighing over five pounds. I had stocked up on soft foods, soups, puddings, and ice cream and he was again eating. But there was a marked difference in his attitude, even in his thought processes.

At first, I thought he was angry with me for having insisted he get dentures. He never would have done that on his own, constantly reminding me that for $15,300.00 he could have bought a new tractor or trailer. But after a couple of days I could see that it was more than just anger. His thinking was foggy. His energy was still depleted. He seemed to be far away most of the time, not really connecting with me on any level. He was absent.

On about the sixth day of his convalescence he woke up and yelled for me to come into the bedroom. Standing by his bed, he had a pained and taut look on his face. "What is this?" he angrily said, almost as if he had found something else he could blame me for. He was holding his abdomen, and when I moved his hand away, his groin was swollen and bulging from underneath his pajamas.

"Oh, no," I muttered, "I *can't believe* this!" Now another condition was crowding into our lives to steal time, and health, and energy, and, of course, money. Money that we didn't have.

"*What?*" Trey yelled. "What the hell *now?*"

"I think it's a hernia, Trey," I explained, using my calmest voice and wanting desperately to convince myself, and him, that it would go away. "You need to go to the doctor. I know they can fix these things. I'll make an appointment."

"Well how did I get it?" he continued. "What did that damned dentist *do* to me?" He was exasperated. I had never seen him lose this much of his temper.

We talked about how he may have strained while under sedation. We thought about over-exertion before the surgery that may have caused it. We ran a hundred scenarios through our thoughts and couldn't settle on any one cause.

"Sometimes things just *are*," I said. "Maybe no one caused it. It just happened." I could tell he was demoralized, and sick of being sick, and tired of worrying about himself. Trey was never one to be sick, not even for one day. Like all tough rancher-types, if he felt bad he'd get up, go to work, and "walk it off." But these months had taken their toll on him.

And I felt very nearly the same way. Just when I had allowed myself to believe that everything would come out all right, that all the aches and pains and weight loss and lack of energy were over, it wasn't. He was angry and I was tired. And scared.

The next day he went to the physician's assistant who had been treating him. The hernia diagnosis was confirmed, and the receptionist told him she'd make an appointment for him with the town's only surgeon. At least, that's what he told me when he got home.

I put him right into bed again and fed him some soup. He said the receptionist would call and let us know when his appointment was with the surgeon. I resigned myself to continuing the ranch chores, keeping food available for Trey to eat, and running our tourist shop. This had by now become the new normal.

Two days later Trey woke up screaming in pain. I ran into his room and tried to calm him down, and made him get back into bed. I elevated his legs with a pillow and that seemed to help some. Since we still had not heard from the receptionist, I ran to the phone and called her.

The receptionist seemed surprised that I had called. She asked how Trey was and when I told her he was not in good shape and wanted to know when our appointment was with the surgeon, she was even more surprised. "Why, that's not *my* job to make the appointment," she answered. Trey was moaning and near crying in the background, and I was on my last nerve.

"That's what you *told* him you would do!" I screamed into the phone. "Now he's in agony and we don't even have an appointment yet! What am I supposed to do *now*? Take him to the emergency room and spend another $2,000 to be told he needs surgery?" I was hysterical. I was furious. I wanted to help my husband's pain to go away. I wanted to go away. The last thing on my mind was that Trey had somehow misinterpreted the receptionist's instruction. I had taken what Trey said at face value and didn't connect his general fogginess with misunderstood instructions. I was righteously, and regrettably, rude.

"Well, I guess so," the receptionist replied with a practiced non-committal voice.

Now losing all of my cool, I think I remember telling her to go to hell and hanging up the phone. I needed to get Trey to the emergency room.

The phone rang within minutes. The physician's assistant was calling to ask what was going on. I told her what had happened and she said she would call the surgeon herself and get Trey an appointment. She apologized profusely. So did I.

I hung up the phone crying.

She called back within ten minutes. Trey now had an appointment with a surgeon who was filling in for the regular surgeon. She said for Trey to take a pain killer and stay in bed until our appointment that afternoon. Thankfully, there was no need for an expensive emergency room visit.

The surgeon again confirmed the diagnosis and told us what to expect from the surgery. She mentioned the approximate cost for her services, and told us to go to the hospital business office for the hospital costs. Her cost alone had already put the surgery out of our reach.

We drove home discussing any option we could think of. Max out another credit card? If nothing else, we had good credit. Borrow from the bank? That could be an option. Now on top of Trey feeling horribly ill, and me feeling sick at heart and overwhelmed by it all, we had to figure out how to get the money, or most of it, up front. I was determined to find some health insurance, somewhere, that we could afford.

It took almost two grueling months, but we finally had the financial dilemma solved. On November 11 Trey was wheeled into a day surgery that would last only about an hour. Recovery should be another two to three hours, and we could go home later that afternoon. He wouldn't need an expensive hospital stay. I waited in his small "day room" after he was taken into the operating room and tried to watch television. Even though I had been reassured that this was a common surgery, I was feeling apprehensive. A nagging feeling sat just beyond my full consciousness, even as I kept reminding myself that this last hurdle would mark a new beginning of health for Trey.

An hour went by. Then two. I was feeling uneasy. The small "day room" was stark and allowed me to begin thinking of all the "what ifs." Thinking of all the horrible and surprising things that can happen when someone is having surgery was consuming me. I willed myself to stop the thoughts and to think only positive thoughts. But three hours later I was worried and upset. About that time, the surgeon walked in.

"We've had some complications," she said, while my stomach seized into a full knot. "I needed to drain over a liter of fluid before I could even begin surgery. Once I got in, I saw his liver and decided to do a biopsy. Here's a picture of his liver."

She handed me a color photo of an organ that appeared to be about half the size of my fist, completely blackened, as if it had been burned. "What does this tell me?" I choked out. I could barely hear my own voice.

"Your husband has stage four cirrhosis," she said in a low, solemn voice.

"How many stages are there?" I whispered. I had to know.

"There are four," she said, with no emotion in her voice.

"So what does this mean?" I heard myself say, noticing that the whole room was seemingly spinning, whirling around me like a dark vortex, dragging me into it whole. I already knew the answers to the questions I was asking but couldn't stop myself from voicing them anyway.

"It means, there is nothing else we can do for him," she said slowly. Then added, "He'll be out of recovery in about an hour and I'm admitting him for, probably, several days to a week. You can wait in his room, and be there when he's brought in. He shouldn't have any more trouble with the hernia. I'll come by tomorrow on my rounds."

And with that everything stopped. I couldn't think. I couldn't

14

speak. I couldn't cry. I couldn't move. I don't think I even breathed. It was a moment in time that hung, suspended, just outside my mind somehow. I pictured myself as if I were a mannequin . . . unmoving, not breathing, with eyes open, still, and unblinking.

I remember finding Trey's room somehow, and waiting there until he was wheeled in, unconscious. He lay there, still as death, and the room was totally silent. Late afternoon sunlight drifted in through the slatted blinds and I lost myself in deep thought.

My mind was rushing forward, considering all of the unbelievable trauma we were both in for. And then again, my thoughts went skipping into the past, reflecting on all the things we had planned to do, all the things that would now be left undone. I couldn't fix Trey. I couldn't fix the ranch. I couldn't fix myself. I sat there and repeated the one comforting thing I could think of: "Be still, and know that I am God." Everything was out of my control.

3

ANOTHER REPRIEVE

THE SECOND DAY IN THE hospital Trey was starting to regain his strength and recover from the surgery. As he seemed to emerge from the anesthesia and the hospital drugs the surgeon visited and went over details of the surgery. She told him she had discovered that he had cirrhosis, but hastily went into more details of the hernia and his projected recovery from that. I could see by the look on Trey's face that the severity of the cirrhosis diagnosis had escaped him. I felt a dark knowing that I would have to face the problem alone, and I would have to be the one to help Trey understand the finality of his diagnosis. If it hadn't been for the intervention of a young and most beautiful nurse, I would have been.

I walked out of Trey's room to take a break as he was getting a breathing treatment. A young, flaming-red haired nurse was waiting outside in the hall. She spoke up without hesitation. "I took the liberty of reading your husband's chart and saw that he has cirrhosis," she said in a voice that reflected experience and belied her youth.

"Well, yes," I responded, and then introduced myself.

Following the best tradition of a small town, she told me her name and then said she was sure I knew her mother, and that she had known Trey since she was a child. "I want you to know," she continued, looking directly into my eyes, "that there is treatment for Trey's condition. There's a group of liver specialists in Dallas, and you should make an appointment for Trey to see them. He can have a liver transplant."

My thoughts started spinning. "She doesn't know we don't have insurance. She doesn't know how serious this is. She doesn't know we have no money for specialists of this kind, let alone a long trip to Dallas. She doesn't know that Trey doesn't know." My disbelief went on and on.

I'm sure she recognized how stunned I was. She offered to get the number for the specialists for me. "Why didn't the doctor tell me this?" I asked when I could recover my voice.

"Oh, I don't know for sure," she answered, "but sometimes the surgeons see patients for the problem they were called in to fix, and then turn them over to their regular doctors. In their defense, I'm sure the trauma they see every day in their regular surgeries tends to prohibit them from getting more closely involved. But I'll be glad to get the information for you and you can take it from there." As she turned to go, she suddenly faced me again and said, "I'll get you the information on the state insurance plan, too . . . in case you may need it."

If this young nurse knew what a lifeline she was throwing out, she didn't act like it. She was upbeat, matter-of-fact, helpful, and all the other attributes of hope in one beautiful package. And, true to her word, she returned within the hour with all the promised information. I told Trey I needed to get back to the ranch and that I would return that evening for dinner with him.

I left feeling like a criminal who has been given the promise of a pardon. I had work to do.

17

4

GOING FOR BROKE

I CALLED THE LIVER SPECIALISTS the next day and was given a referral to one of the doctors in the group. Fortunately, the Dallas specialists had an outreach clinic in Odessa, only two hours away from us. Thankfully a trip to Dallas was avoidable. The first available appointment was two and a half months away. I reserved the appointment, and counted my lucky stars that I was able to get it. Convincing Trey to go would be a much harder job.

Returning to the hospital, I told Trey about the nurse, the specialists, and the certainty that he could be "fixed." He didn't buy it.

"We don't need to do that," he said, again relying on the practiced denial of reality that had always come in so handy for him.

"Yes, we need it!" I fairly yelled, as if talking louder would make the situation clearer.

"We don't have the kind of money it would take to have a liver transplant," he continued in a too matter-of-fact voice. "That's just ridiculous. That's the kind of thing you see in the movies."

"Well we can find the money," I said in desperation, talking faster now instead of louder, with the same dismal results. "I can sell some of my stock. Maybe your brother would let us sell some of the ranch. There are all kinds of things we can try. We can't just give up! People don't die in America because they don't have enough money to get fixed!"

I told him I had already made an appointment for February, and we could talk over the details between now and then. I could see he was too tired, and too sick, to continue the argument. And I could see the thin film of denial starting to disappear in his eyes. I didn't want to belabor the point. I didn't want to come right out and tell him he was dying and would be gone within months if we didn't do something. I didn't want to add my worry and fear to his already severe illness. Actually, I didn't want to face the reality, myself.

And so he leaned back into his hospital bed and closed his eyes. I held his hand and watched the filtered sunlight through the blinds grow dimmer as the day progressed. I tried not to think about the future. I tried not to think about the unthinkable. I tried not to think about the effort it would take to get Trey to the specialist. Somehow I was conscious enough to know that all I wanted to do was put Trey's hand on my face. To listen to his soft breathing and watch his pale face regain some color as the hours marched by. I wanted to savor the moment. I told myself that later I could look back on this moment and see that I had prevailed and we had done the right thing. In my fantasy projection we were laughing because we had thought Trey would die. We were delirious with the reprieve of living and loving each other for an infinite amount of time. We were childishly oblivious to the human condition of time.

Visiting hours were over and I drove back to the ranch in darkness, a million things in a list of what I should do: fix soup and other soft dishes for Trey to eat when he got home, make his bed comfortable so that he would stay in it long enough for his surgery to heal, buy treats and "comfort food" for his nightstand, have magazines and the tv remote handy, buy new pajamas – the silk ones that he liked – so he wouldn't get dressed, arrange for someone to help me in the shop so I could be available for Trey, finish the application(s) for insurance coverage, call my broker and see about selling what little stock I had. The list was seemingly endless.

Trey and I had agreed on one thing. We would tell no one of his condition. He didn't want to worry family members. The death of his father two years prior was still fresh in everyone's memory and he didn't want to add to the sadness and worry. I agreed because I know that when people are apprised of dangerous situations it is natural to think the worst, and what we didn't need was a whole host of folks projecting bad, worried energy into the situation. We needed good energy. We needed hope. We needed a miracle.

5

WHEEL OF FORTUNE

TREY CAME HOME FROM THE hospital, the days turned into weeks, and his recovery from surgery resolved seamlessly. He had lost even more weight, and he didn't have his strength back, but he was up and feeding cattle, checking fence lines, and generally feeling better, even while tiring quickly.

We had kept our promise to each other not to tell anyone about his condition, and so we waited for the February appointment in guarded silence between us.

The day arrived for us to drive the two-hour stint to see the specialist in Odessa. Always nervous when I had to go to an unknown place at an appointed time in a city with traffic, we left early. It was February 12.

I was relieved that the weather was good and I didn't have to contend with snow, ice, rain or wind. In fact, I recall it was somewhat balmy. The sun was out and the sky was that vivid blue that only Texas can produce. Trey's eyes were the same hue.

I took it as a sign of good luck when I was able to find the medical building the outreach liver specialists used for our area.

We found a parking space, and walked almost two blocks up to the building, half of which was under construction. The sign on the outside of the building said "Cancer Outreach Program" or something to that effect. I remember thinking that we must be in the wrong place. Trey didn't have cancer. I looked more closely and a small sign indicated that this was, indeed, the area for liver specialists. We stopped just short of the doors, both of us thinking that this was quite the momentous event. I took a deep breath and we walked inside.

The room was packed. Row after row of people sat silently watching the newcomers walk in. A small television set was perched above the crowd and a few people were watching the mindless daytime programming. The chairs were arranged to make room for walkers, wheel chairs, and canes. Caregivers, the obvious well-ones, sat next to pale and mostly listless patients. I wanted to throw up.

We walked to the reception area, I signed Trey in, and handed over the pertinent medical and insurance papers. We took a seat at the very far end of the waiting room, unconsciously wanting to distance ourselves from the *really* sick patients. We weren't sick. Trey just had cirrhosis. He didn't have cancer. Cirrhosis is cured with a liver transplant; take out the bad liver, put a new and healthy one in. Trey wasn't sick. His liver was bad.

Trey looked nervous. In an effort to both have something to do and make him feel better, I offered to make us a cup of coffee or hot chocolate in the small refreshment room facing us. He was grateful and as we sat silently drinking our fake hot chocolate in Styrofoam cups, I remember thinking, "Thank GOD Trey doesn't have cancer. These people look awful."

After about an hour of waiting we were ushered in to a small room. It was furnished with a tiny desk, a chair for the doctor, two chairs for others, and a small examining table. The lighting was harsh and bright, reflecting glare off the white polished floors. Shortly a man of approximately late sixties in age, dressed in casual pants and shirt, walked in. He introduced himself, shook our hands and sat down at the desk.

He asked a few questions, went over the paperwork from the hernia surgeon, and wasted no time in giving short answers to our obviously unwanted questions. It was clear he didn't want conversation. He asked Trey to get on the examining table and unbutton his shirt. A cursory examination, palpating his stomach, looking at eyes, nose and throat, and he was done. He told Trey to dress and get back off the table, while he simultaneously wrote notes in his paperwork, his back to us.

The man was curt and rude. He made several unkind remarks that were characteristically missed by Trey, but not by me. About the time I was ready to let him know I was not pleased, the doctor wheeled his chair around and faced us.

In a clipped tone he told Trey that by his estimation he was about a 9 or 10 on the scale of needing a liver transplant. He continued by saying that one had to be at least a twenty before being considered for a new liver. He went on to say that if Trey ate right, got exercise and rest, and quit smoking, it could be up to two years before his liver was bad enough for a transplant. I was suddenly starting to like this man more and more. Even though he was personally rude, the message he had for us was glorious. I quickly decided to forgive him his horrible bedside manner.

Trey's abdomen was quite distended. I asked if we should have the fluid drained. "Yes, probably," he allowed, and went on to say that "In the old days a doctor could just palpate the abdomen and see where to place the drain tube. Nowadays they'll want to do a sonogram to make sure they get it right and don't get sued." He instructed us to go home, go to our regular doctor, have the sonogram and if fluid needed to be drained, the hometown doctor would do it. He said he'd see us in six months, and unceremoniously got up and started to leave. He stopped just short of the door, then turned and looked at Trey.

"How old did you say you are?" he blurted out.

"I'm 54," Trey quietly answered.

"Huh." He said with a surprised look on his face. "You look a lot older," he said mindlessly. And with that, he opened the door and left the room.

Trey and I sat silently stunned while we tried to ignore his rudeness and think about the good news. Conflicting emotions of unmitigated joy at Trey's prognosis, and festering hurt at the doctor's demeanor left me momentarily speechless. Running over all the doctor's information in my head I realized that we had at least a couple of years before even getting to the liver transplant part, and by then medical advances would surely make the whole procedure even easier, while giving us time to find the money to have it done.

Life was good. Trey was smiling. We held hands walking out the long corridor, feeling relief beyond measure. One quick trip to the lab for some prescribed blood tests and we were headed home. Sweet time stretched before us like an endless highway.

6

A QUICK DECLINE

WE MADE AN APPOINTMENT WITH our primary doctor to have the fluid in Trey's abdomen assessed. The appointment wasn't until the end of February and on March 1 we went back to the doctor to find out if the fluid procedure was necessary.

As we waited in a small and horribly crowded waiting room, I thought about all the different doctors we'd been to, all the waiting rooms we'd sat in, and wondered how many more were in our future. Sure, Trey was only 54 years old, but it felt as if we'd suddenly been thrust into a geriatric population of endless doctors' visits, and relentless conversations about this or that ailment. Finally it was our turn to see the doctor.

I could tell by the look on his face that the doctor was carefully choosing how to say what he had to say. His posture was tight, and while he glanced from me to to Trey, he never really looked either of us directly in the eye.

I watched Trey's amiable smile slowly fade when the doctor said, "Trey, the sonogram picked up something in the picture that I'm not quite sure about. I'd like for you to have a CAT scan so that I can get a better look. I've made an appointment for you to have the scan today, if you can drive on out to the hospital and have it done."

With those words another round of dread set in. Trey looked confused. "So, you don't want to have the fluid drained today?" he asked, still not quite sure of what the doctor had said.

As caregivers learn to do, I quickly jumped in and told the doctor that of course we'd have the CAT scan done that day. I made an appointment for the following week to come back in and get the results.

Was it my imagination that the receptionist wouldn't look at me when she made the appointment for the following week? Was she speaking in barely a whisper? Were those tears in Trey's eyes? Reality had taken another sudden turn into a dizzying cacophony of indecipherable messages. I hurried Trey out of the building, into the car, and we headed toward the hospital.

My mind racing, I told Trey that this would be a test that wouldn't be painful, but would give us a clearer picture of what the liver doctor had said. I repeated that we shouldn't worry, but rather focus on the fact that he was getting such good medical care, with up-to-date tests. I chattered away, saying anything I could think of, that would stop my mind, and hopefully his, from feeling the sudden fear of impending disaster.

After the CAT scan we returned to the ranch. I was so anxiety ridden I decided I could not wait until the following week for the results of the scan. I called our doctor's office to see if they would have the results earlier than that. Without hesitation the receptionist said that yes, I should come in on Thursday. "You mean tomorrow? You'll have the results by then?" I asked incredulously. "Yes," she said softly, and I did not question her beyond that, but felt a lessening of the anxiety and worry about waiting for the results.

That night Trey and I snuggled close as we talked about the days to come, and what the tests might reveal. "I don't mind dying," I remember him saying, "but I just don't want to leave you." I made the wrong response, and one I'll regret forever. Instead of letting us both have a conversation about dying, I quickly said that he "wasn't going to die." I reminded him of the liver specialists' prognosis. I told him dying was way down the line. I told him I was almost ten years older than he and I would die first. I told him we would go through this together, and be the stronger for it. We cried, and quit talking.

As we walked into the doctor's office on Thursday it felt like a ton of weight descended on us. The doctor was clearly upset, his eyes moist, his speech slow and faltering. "Trey," he started, "You've been dealt a really unfair hand. You have liver cancer, and it has spread to your adrenals, your gall bladder, and other organs. I'm so sorry."

Trey stared straight ahead and sat ramrod stiff. "Well, I don't want chemotherapy or radiation or any of that crap," he said through the tears beginning to well in his eyes. "Just let nature take its course."

The doctor looked at me and saw that, even if Trey didn't, I understood that there was no treatment to be given. He looked back at Trey and said in a measured tone, "You don't have to have anything you don't want. We'll do it just the way you want it."

By now we were all crying. I asked how long we had. The doctor replied that there was no way to know, but possibly six weeks, maybe six months. We collected ourselves and walked out of the room. As we passed the receptionist, this time she did have tears in her eyes and she did not look up, but busied herself with paperwork on her desk.

That was a Thursday. Trey felt badly on Friday, and I assumed it was because of the devastating news. He stayed in bed all day.

On Saturday, he died.

7

HELP

THE FINALITY OF TREY'S DEATH became a shroud that covered me completely for the next two months. I talked, and walked and worked as if I were sleepwalking, drifting in and out of a strange twilight that kept my world dark no matter the dazzling sunlight of spring. Friends and family called, friends and family came by to see me, adjoining ranchers came to tell me they would feed our cows as long as I needed them to, as well as look out for problems out in the pastures. At such encounters I would try to act "normal," and try to "remember my manners," and try to be grateful, and try not to let anyone know that I didn't know who I was anymore or what I should be doing. Basically, I followed a script. Smile on cue. Say "thank you." Offer a comforting hug when someone breaks down. Be strong. All the conditioned responses I had learned in my birth family came into play.

Even the ones I knew, deep down through my fog, to be wrong.

My father arrived to "help" me. He stayed for seven weeks. He became the authority again, calling the shots for every emerging catastrophe. As dirty dishes claimed all the space in the kitchen, he decided I needed a dishwasher. I tried to explain we didn't have the water pressure we would need for one to work properly. No matter, he knew I needed one and was determined I have one. "I'm going to help you pay for things," he said, "so don't worry about that." And so, I bought a new dishwasher.

The plumber arrived to install the new dishwasher, only to find out the gas hot water heater was ancient, and sat in a small unvented hall closet. He refused to do any further work until I bought a new one, and installed it in a larger, and vented, laundry room. "I'm going to help you!" my father assured me. "Go ahead and buy one and let's get this dishwasher installed!" And so, I paid for the new water heater. Then the plumber told me he only hooked up the dishwasher. He didn't do the carpentry work needed to install it under the counter top. I paid for the carpenter. Once that was done, the plumber came back and installed the thing. I paid the plumber. Finally, everything was installed, and so began the washer's maiden voyage. Unbelievably, that's when the entire water system quit working.

Still moving ghostlike through whatever endeavor I was told to engage in, I walked from the well to the house, from the house to the well, checking electrical boxes, looking at gauges, checking valves, looking for water breaks, and trying to find where the buried water line went. After more than a week of no water, my father again commandeered the problem. "You've got to get this fixed!" he yelled. "Don't you understand? Don't you know that Trey's DEAD! HE'S DEAD and he's never coming back! Get this fixed!" I was so lost in the fog, I didn't even cry.

Dad had no experience with water wells or with the companies that work on wells. There were two such companies in the whole of Brewster County. It was springtime, when EVERYONE with a well needed work done. We would have to "get in line," I was told by both companies. "RIDICULOUS!" my father shouted. "Call an electrician! Call a plumber! Call those two ranch hands who came by the other day. I'll bet they'll know how to fix it!" An electrician and a ranch hand came out to see if they could help. To their credit, they worked well into the night by the light of a lantern and with the help of a full moon. They finally called it quits and we all went into the house.

"How much do I owe you?" I asked the electrician. "Honestly Ma'am, I hate to charge you anything. I didn't fix your problem." My father was standing behind him, and held up five fingers. "Would five hundred be all right?" I asked. He nodded yes and thanked me. I wrote out a check for him, and five hundred more for his helper, believing my father would help with this, too, as he had promised.

Eventually the well company came out and fixed the problem. It was none too soon, as summer was fast approaching, and taking showers at the cabins was becoming more and more of a chore. Not to mention hauling jugs of drinking water. And, eventually, Dad thought everything was in order and it would be safe for him to leave. His parting words were, "I've written a check to you for $1,200 . . . that should cover it."

Relieved that he was finally leaving I didn't want to jinx his departure by saying anything more than, "Thank you." After all, it was just one more horrible event in my world of horrible events. The summer rolled on, my fog slowly lessened, and each day brought me a little closer to the realization that I had to live my own life. And I had to live it without Trey.

8

OCTOBER

So now it's fall, and I find myself doing what I do every fall and it feels wrong. Wrong because this fall is different from all the others I've known. Wrong because this fall it makes me sad instead of feeling giddy to unwrap all the now forgotten clothes I put away last spring. Wrong because all of these clothes fit another lifetime, another lifestyle, another size, another life.

Trey used to laugh at me at my change of season ritual. He wore the same clothes in every season. Like a uniform, warm in winter and cool in summer. He was into layers, and that worked well in the high desert. Undershirt to wick away moisture, long sleeved shirt to shield the sun, vests for winter, and hats for Summer. Jeans. Boots. A lesson in simplicity that I never learned.

This is another first-time activity since Trey's death. I hate it. I want to pick out one outfit and wear it every day and never have to face a "first" again. I'm sick from the duel between having to move on and wanting to my life to be the way it was. It permeates everything now. Everything I do or don't do must first be processed by the "Staying or Going Machine." It's maddening.

9

ANXIETY ATTACK

IT'S THE FIRST TIME I'VE felt really pressed by someone wanting to buy the ranch. Hell, it's not even near being on the market yet. Until today, that was just some far off option that "might" happen. Until today, I could feel content to think I had some plan in mind, should I move away. Until today, there was some feeling of having someplace to go "after the ranch." Buyers called who have more than enough money to buy the ranch. They wanted to drive all the way back from Del Rio just to see it. They wanted to come for the garage sale. They wanted to see if there was something that should stay with the ranch that they should buy. They sounded as if they knew that they would, indeed, one day have this ranch. They wanted to come just after the garage sale. They pressed and pressed. They asked if they should turn around and drive right back here *TONIGHT* to see the ranch tomorrow. Even when I told them I'd have no information about selling until December, they pressed.

I fixed a drink. My favorite. I sat in the hot tub. I listened to calming music. I sat on the patio. I cried. Then I started looking at real estate on the internet. Kerrville, Corpus Christi, Comfort, Rockport, Costa Rica, hell I even looked at Victoria. No house looked like mine. No condo looked like home. I wondered why I wanted to be on the coast. I don't have a boat, I don't even like riding in someone else's boat. I don't like the humidity. The places all looked like someone else's life. The houses were cluttered and chopped up. I cried again. Where would I want to be, when I can be anywhere? Nowhere. You cannot buy a life. You cannot buy a feeling of familiarity. You cannot end one chapter of your life and jump happily into another. You can't recreate yourself, just because you have money.

I think everything is moving too fast. I have to have time to process everything that is happening to me. The phone rings and from across the ether and someone I don't know is telling me perhaps they should come to my garage sale because they may need to buy something that should stay on the ranch. They spoke as if they were assured of being the buyers. They spoke as if they were assured that I was going to sell. They spoke fast. They jumped from one idea to the next as if being in a hurry would help to pin me down.

And then later, on this lonely October night, on tonight of all nights, no one else called. Tonight of all nights, no one came over. Tonight of all nights, there was nothing to do that had to be done. In short, tonight was the perfect petri dish in which to grow anxiety.

My thoughts rambled around like static on a bad radio station. I don't want to go, but I can't stay. I am too isolated here. It is too expensive here. That is what I've been telling myself. Maybe I can stay just a little longer. Maybe I can stay just long enough to let go.

10

GARAGE SALE

IT'S BEEN AT LEAST TWO months' worth of work. First planning
"when" . . . fitting in when my friends can help, finding a date that
isn't taken up by five other things, giving myself time to get it all
together. I decide on Nov. 3, 4, and 5. That's the last stable date in
the fall when I can more or less depend on the weather cooperating
so that it isn't cold, isn't hot, isn't windy . . . hopefully.

Then the cleanup begins. The warehouse hasn't been touched
in years. It's filthy. I can't even get to the "stuff" before cleaning it.
I forget to wear a mask. I breathe in rat shit, bat shit, dust, dirt,
oil and grime. I haul out massive barrels of trash, load them on
the pickup, drive down to the dumpster, pick the barrel up again,
dump it in, and take the empty back. By night my back, hernia, legs
and feet are in spasms. By the next day, I am hacking up the results
of breathing in such an environment. I continue.

Finally the room is clean enough, and enough space is cleared
to begin bringing out the "treasures." They are filthy. I begin to
clean everything . . . again. During that process, I make more
cleaning necessary on the room itself. I force myself to go on, in

an exhausting dance of moving, cleaning, moving, and cleaning. I cajole my friends to help me. I pay people to help me. I barter with people to help me. The dance goes on and on, until one fine day, all the "stuff" of garage sale dreams is lined up orderly, priced with small white tags, and waiting silently to be "just the thing" for some new owner. I wonder how I'm going to feel, when I watch small pieces of my life, small pieces of Trey's life, walk away in the arms of some new lover. It makes me cry to think of it.

But today, it is almost Halloween. Everyone seems giddy with sugared up festive spirit. The deer hunters are here, immersed in their anticipation of returning at Thanksgiving to have their annual hunt. Tourists are thick as flies, rejoicing in the perfect weather and finding the perfect treasure out on the ranch. The final phases of the sale are beginning their countdown. All that is left to do is to get the ad on the radio and in the newspapers, answer telephone calls, and put the final touches on the outside of the house. I have four days until the pieces walk off.

"Make yourself familiar with the angels, and behold them frequently in spirit; for without being seen, they are present and with you."

St. Francis de Sales

Even though it's only three days until the sale, and I am hard pressed to get everything ready, I had to take the time to clean my house today. I had to make at least one part of my house feel like my house. I spend valuable garage sale time cleaning my bedroom, bath, and den. Finally, I clear a small refuge. Friends contact me and have fallen ill . . . unable to help with the sale. Other friends contact me and offer to help. What a miraculous thing, this living is. So up, so down. The dance has become a frenzied whirlwind of unexpected emotions, unexpected tragedies, unexpected gifts.

My sister-in-law arrives, her mother-in-law in tow. They are 3 days early for the sale. As they look in the nooks and crannies of the heap on my living room floor, I start to feel my stomach doing flip-flops. She begins a tentative conversation. I feel an unease that is more just a sense of something to come, rather than something tangible. And then, she just asks outright for me to return my wedding ring to her. The ring had been one of her mother's rings. It was the only thing of his mother's that Trey had ever asked her for, and then he had proposed to me with it, offering it as a symbol of the circle our lives had become. I'll never forget the moment. We parked on the county road leading to the ranch, looking directly at a gorgeous sunset, the backdrop behind Cathedral Mountain. How perfect. I didn't know he was such a romantic. He was as nervous as a schoolboy. He said he had loved me forever. He said, "Will you marry me? Will you make my life perfect?" And then we both cried. We cried with happiness that our roads had finally merged at the right time. We cried for the years we had lost. We cried.

And now his sister was rewriting history. She was telling me the ring had only been a loan; telling me that as Trey lay dying, and she told me to keep it, she didn't mean keep it *forever*. Now she would like to have it back, "when you're ready," she added to make it sound like kindness, as if I would EVER be ready to give away those memories of Trey. It was a mean moment, hanging there above us both, as she tried to make it sound okay that she would ask such a thing. I was too astonished to even speak. I let her request twist silently there in the empty space between us as I stared into her eyes. I wondered if she knew what she was saying. I wondered if she had any idea of what it is like to lose the one person so precious in your life. I wondered how she had convinced herself that it would be all right to say these things to me. Finally, she broke the silence and said slowly, as if I were too stupid to understand her request, "If you are going to sell it, I'd like to buy it." The last and lowest blow. I walked away.

11

THANKSGIVING

Once it finally dawned on me that Thanksgiving and Christmas holidays had not been cancelled because of my despair, the dread began. For weeks vague scenarios stuck in the back of my mind, refusing to take form. Little by little I began to feel pressed to "make plans." Did I want to be alone on Thanksgiving? Did I want to be with people? Did I want to eat my pain away? What did I want? The only constant in my life seemed to be the ever-present questions that needed to be made clear.

I made plans. Then I re-made the plans. Then I decided I'd just stay at home. Then I re-made the plans I had made in the first place, and vowed to keep them. I was going to my friends' house for a glorious Thanksgiving feast.

I did keep my plans, and it was a quite nice day. It dawned in that spectacular fashion that only a Texas fall day can; brilliant baby blue sky, full sun, no clouds, no wind, everything golden and blue and crisp. My friends were so loving and so kind, and there was no hint of anything sad. The day passed and became evening, and a delicious blue norther was beginning to blow in.

I left and came home to watch the last University of Texas vs. Texas A&M football game there would ever be. (Yeah right, like THAT'S gonna happen!) This game had been a required ritual in my house since I was a small child, and I wasn't going to let this year be any different. To complete my rare good mood, Texas even won the game and would go down for all posterity as the superior team. And, by some strange association, that meant that all their supporters, me especially, would enjoy that cloak of superiority.

But it all took so much effort; emotional effort. It's very hard to force yourself NOT to think about something. And by early the next day, aptly named Black Friday, I was weak and tired and worried and frenzied all over again. I went to town to do a few chores, and to get ready for my trip to Corpus the following week. But mainly I went just because I needed something to do.

Coming home, the tiny thought I wouldn't let myself think, finally birthed itself. I've noticed for some time now that every time I drive down the county lane to my house, a huge, bleak sadness overcomes me. I am coming home to an empty house. I am coming home to unloading my car all by myself, again. I am coming home to find something to do that doesn't remind me that I am about to fall off the earth, again. It is exhausting to stay busy enough not to think. And so today, Black Friday, I rode down that lane again, and it was even raining . . . well, drizzling, and I had an Eagles cd playing . . . "I been tryin' to get down, to the heart of the matter, but the flesh is weak, and my thoughts start to scatter, but I think it's about, forgiveness, forgiveness . . ."

Forgiveness. Now there is a re-occurring theme in my life, I thought. I needed to actually *practice* forgiveness. It needed to be something I *did* not just something I *said*. "Just exactly what *is* forgiveness?" I wondered. Does the whole concept imply *fault* or *blame*? Was it Trey's fault that he died? Was it my fault I couldn't

39

love him enough to save him? Was it some God's fault that people couldn't be immortal? Denial of our mortality may be the biggest American illusion, a deluded habit of thinking that sets us up to experience shock at some point in our brief existence. Somehow, we live our lives, going day to day, acting as if there will always be a tomorrow. Sometimes there is no tomorrow. Sometimes, we are not in control.

And, of course, control is what it's all about. We have to deny there is death to be able to believe we control our lives; to believe that what we do, what we say, and what we think is actually controllable; that it's not just some rote, memorized, mechanical, knee-jerk activity. By believing we will never die, we are assured of having time to correct mistakes, to "get it right next time." A certain level of accountability is gone. There will always be time to do better.

I wanted to forgive myself for believing that Trey would never die. I wanted to forgive Trey for *letting* me believe that. And like a lot of other things, I realized that forgiveness is not a single act, but a practice, a way of living. William Paul Young said, "If anything matters, then everything matters. Because you are important, everything you do is important. Every time you forgive, the universe changes; every time you reach out and touch a heart or a life, the world changes. With every kindness, seen or unseen, nothing will be the same again." The practice, itself, is a way of waking up, of pulling myself out of denial. And once out, how do I keep myself from sinking back *into* denial?

Somehow, I think the key is that I have to remember who I am now, who I have been throughout my life, and who I want to become. I have to keep myself as a touchstone. "I am important, so everything I do is important."

And so, I decided to take out my guitar again . . . after all these years. After putting away that part of myself again for 10 long years and letting the songs I wrote become barely remembered, I knew I had to revisit who I was. If I could start to remember who I was, maybe there would be a way to regain who I am. And then, maybe, a way to become who I want to be on this strange and new journey alone.

12

CORPUS CHRISTI

THE TRIP WAS EYE-OPENING, IF nothing else. Even though I thought I was organized and ready to leave, it's a struggle to actually get something completed, by myself. The deer hunters informed me they would be leaving Tuesday also to hunt in another location. Now I had to find new pet sitters on the spur of the moment. Of course, friends came to my rescue . . . again. That task taken care of, I concentrated on what to take. Somehow, I always take the wrong stuff. This trip was no different. Finally, the morning arrived and I left the ranch early. A two hour drive to Odessa-Midland got me to my flight with time to spare. Then the flight to Dallas, where the only seat was next to two "chatty Cathy's" who never took a breath. Then on to Houston, where an enormous man in a flannel shirt sat next to me and sneezed, sans handkerchief, all the way. By that time I was starving and forced myself to eat a salad at Papadeux's and drink a beer. All by myself. Maybe that doesn't sound like such a feat, but for me, it was. For my adult life, going alone into a restaurant was not something I could do. And sit at a bar, alone? That wouldn't happen. But here it was, happening. The salad was good, the waiter was nice, the beer was cold. I let myself enjoy it.

By the time I got to Corpus I could feel I was "coming down" with something. My friends, Bill and Dennis, met me at the Corpus airport. They took one look at me and said we would be going to their doctor the next day. In the meantime they bundled me up in a cashmere throw, propped a cashmere pillow behind my head, and promptly took me to their home. The next day, true to their word, they took me to their doctor, where a true miracle happened. The walls of the waiting room were lined with patients. Every chair was taken. I gave a little information to the receptionist, and POOF! I was escorted into a private room. I didn't even have time to sit down. The nurse took my history, took my vital signs, and gave me a shot. Then, POOF! We were back in the waiting room where I was informed I would be billed, and that the doctor would see me at his other clinic where he did outpatient procedures on Thursdays. When I arrived at that office I was taken immediately into an exam room and the doctor came in within five minutes. He did a quick upper respiratory exam, gave me two prescriptions, and told me he thought I'd live. All of it took less than an hour. With sudden clarity I realized that the medical care I had been receiving for well on ten years, was sub-par, cursory, at best a pat on the head, and often dangerous. I was just so used to the poor medical situation in my small town I had begun to think it was medical care, when in fact it had very little to do with anything medical, and nothing at all to do with care. Note to self: live somewhere that has good medical options and quit acting like it doesn't matter.

13

HOLIDAYS

NOTHING LIKE THE MONTH OF December to dampen your spirits and make you crazy. The American dream has so informed us of the myths of the season, I don't understand how anyone can get through this month without wanting to commit suicide or worse. It's like the whole month is shrouded in cake icing. Sugary sweet, nostalgic, eye-popping visuals, a carnival of well-known songs . . . it's all just too much. And then, of course, life doesn't stop for the season. You still have to work and make money, you still have to balance your checkbook, pay bills, buy groceries, take phone calls, send emails . . . but it's like it's all done on steroids. This year, I just want it to be over. And I'm not normally a "bah Humbug!" type of person. Let's just say that this year my vision has cleared. I can now see through the fluff and fancy of it all.

And then, of course, me being me, I have to feel guilty about feeling that way. Just today I learned that my old friend, Evelyn, a single woman who was a rancher for generations in the West Texas desert, died last weekend. She doesn't get to feel one way or the other about this Christmas. At least her family will have their first

Christmas without her without having to plan for it for a year, as if that's a consolation. They won't have to wait months to establish that milestone. Me, on the other hand, I've waited ten months for yet another "first" since Trey's death. But the guilt is there, just the same. It's terrible to feel guilty for being alive when others aren't. But that's the bottom line.

In the days immediately following Trey's death I thought about how life is like those awful science fiction movies of the fifties. You knew the monster was coming to get you, just like we know that death is coming to us all. But somehow, somehow we manage to put the thought away. We don't live every moment knowing it may be our last. We don't celebrate every holiday thinking we may never see another one. It takes the actual death of someone very close to you to bring that knowing to the forefront of your existence.

Now I see that the ever-present reality of death cuts through the fakery that Christmas has become, blinding me with the duality. I am hopeful that this "stage" will pass. I am yearning to be my "self" again. Somewhere deep inside I know that the only way to make this shocking revelation of death subside is to live.

14

GETTING READY FOR GRIEF

AGAIN, THE DAY DAWNED GRAY and dreary, but with no rain. (I think God has issued an edict that it will never rain in Brewster County again.) I needed something to do until the evening, when I would go to my first ever "grief group" meeting. It will probably only be two of us, but you never know. I decided to cook a dinner for some favorite and faithful friends, Sharon and Al. Sharon's cat of 23 years died and she is mourning her fur baby, and of course having to work, too. And so, I took out the last four beef ribs from the steer Trey and I raised, looked up a recipe for potatoes au gratin, made a quick cranberry relish and I was done. It still wasn't even noon.

To pass the time I decided to make my Christmas fudge, or at least one pan of it. I'll take a plate of it to the bank, another to the CPA, one to Sharon and Al. I'll probably have to make another batch. I always think of someone to take a plate to that I had forgotten about. And that reminds me . . . one to my hair salon. And then it was time to get ready to go to the meeting.

15

GRIEF GROUP

SITTING SAFELY WITH AT LEAST one other person, with soft candlelight and a glass of wine, I was surprised at my first glimpse of allowing myself to see how deep these emotions are going to go. For ten months I have been so busy taking care of everyone else, keeping the ranch together, trying to make a little money to pay bills, I had only intermittent spells of time to grieve; very intermittent. But sitting with my new friend, Renee, who is a widow, herself, and knows exactly what I'm talking about (even when I don't) is so heart-opening. She is a lovely person and if ever anyone had an 800 number to God, she does.

We talked about what she called, "complicated grief." It's not just that my husband died, it's that previous trauma has an enormous role to play in my situation. Feeling like I am "back to square one" in the middle of this big empty desert, alone, losing my identity (again), my livelihood (again), my house (again), my loved one . . . well, it's complicated. Now all the emotions from the long ago trauma swell up along with the grief of losing Trey. Getting word that Evelyn died hasn't helped. The sight of her ranch as I sat atop a mountain in the desert on one far-away and fateful night kept me sane. Her pioneer spirit and military courage seemed to jump into me during the horrible events of that night, and somehow I survived.

And then, too, it's this season of Christmas. I have never had such repressed depression. I can't let myself "go." Someone will call. Someone will come to the shop. A neighbor will stop by. I am keeping everything safely tucked away in a box to be opened, "someday." Opened someday when I can hide from the world. Opened someday when I believe I'm strong enough to feel what's inside. Opened someday when I can survive the impact.

16

A LONG TIME COMING

I'VE DONE EVERYTHING I CAN think of to do. I've made two batches of fudge, one pan of pralines, two different kinds of Christmas cookies, a batch of "Texas trash," and cheese/sausage balls. I've delivered goods to friends and businesses. I've been to two small parties, had drinks, exchanged gifts. I've cleaned the shop. I've cleaned the heritage museum. I've cleaned the house. I've made lists for New Year's Eve. I've planned menus. All of this and STILL Christmas is a week away. I'm tired of trying to get through it. Tired is the right word. All of the above takes energy. A lot of energy. Maybe I'm just old. I look old. I feel old. I act like I'm coping when anyone is around. I stay upbeat when anyone calls. I am a lie.

I just want the world to go back to normal. It never will. It never was.

17

A COLD NIGHT

It never got over 20 degrees all day. A misty want-to-snow day that kept me inside all day. Even my dog, Buddy, only made it outside a couple of times. I busied myself, as usual, with things that needed to be done for next week. Futuring. Not living today because I can't bear it . . . as if keeping my mind on tomorrow, next week, next year, I'll get through today. My visual is one of a boat making it to the opposite shore by means of pulling on a rope stretched across the gulf. I pull and pull and if I pull hard enough, I'll get there.

I washed clothes so I could use the dryer to help keep the house warm. When all the clothes were washed, including Buddy's doggie blankets, I forgot to leave water on somewhere. Around 7:00 I tried to wash some dishes . . . no water. Frantic I ran to the bathroom and turned on tub and sink faucets and tried to flush the toilet. No water. I ran to the "sunroom" thinking the hose to the plant room is insulated and would still have running water. No such luck. I don't know about the magic of "things." If no water runs, do pipes burst? Does the pump stop working? What about the cabins? With visitors coming in 3 days will there be water there? It's all too much to think about. I don't know how to run this house. I don't know how to run this ranch. I am so anxiety ridden over being expected to do things I don't know how to do, and even if I did know how, I wouldn't be capable of doing whatever was necessary. It's a horrible feeling. Like being stranded on an island completely alone and anything that gets done gets done by only you.

I had lunch yesterday with another widow . . . a long time friend who has since remarried after the death of her husband. We chatted about nothing and had nice sandwiches and tea. As we were leaving she asked how I was "doing." Fine, I lied, pasting the same old half smile across my face and hoping she'd buy it. She didn't. "It does get better," she said. "I know it's horrible now, but it does get better." I felt the tears beginning to well up and made a quick good-bye, with well wishes for a Merry Christmas. So incongruous. But I just couldn't talk about it anymore. Talking about being alone makes it too real.

This weather is getting scary. For the second year in a row we have record breaking freezes. This old house is not built for such severe weather. Heat is fine. But these low temperatures make everything unworkable. I turned on the living room lights to check the water in the sunroom. I accidentally turned on the ceiling fan, and now it won't turn off. Weird. Why? I don't know, but I told myself that the universe turned the fan on to circulate the higher, and warmer, air throughout the room, since I was obviously too dense to think of that. Thank you, universe. I'm glad you're in charge and not me.

18

CHRISTMAS EVE DAY

LISTENING TO HILARY STAGG'S "THINKING OF YOU" on the Sirius music station, I try to keep my thoughts from wandering into depression. In an effort to save power, and money, only the music and the computer are on. Buddy sleeps at my feet, the cat purring atop the couch, and a blanket of beautiful snow outside the windows. Even not having water is bearable because I am cocooned in a warm room, with angelic music, loving pets, and a picture book scene outside. I force myself to forget that the only thing missing is Trey.

I'm tempted to put on all my outside clothes and go for a walk. I wish I had a camera. It will probably be my last Christmas here on the ranch. I am blessed that it is so perfect. What opposites exist in my reality. I can feel bleak because of all the things I've lost and am now losing, or I can feel blessed for the way everything is.

My choice.

It gets down to accepting that it's MY CHOICE.

I'm going for a walk.

19

THE WALK

I PUT ON TWO PAIR of my thickest socks and wore Trey's fur lined
suede boots that came up almost to my knees. I gave them to him
for Christmas probably eight years ago, and liked them so much
I bought myself a pair the next year. But mine are shorter and I try
to just wear them in the house. His are just right with the extra
socks. Then I put on his huge camouflage coat, wrapped a wool
scarf around my neck, insulated mittens, a cap, and Buddy and
I were ready to go.

Outside it looked dreary and gray. Spots of bare ground were
muddy and not covered with snow. Buddy was glad to be out and
have something to do, but I was hard pressed to think of some
place to walk where the view wasn't one of a wrecked life. So many
generations had passed through the ranch. The litter of all those
generations of long-gone people scattered about, some in piles,
some just forgotten, cast an eerie feeling. I didn't like it at all but
walked anyway just for the exercise.

Then I remembered that I really needed to go to the cabin at
the creek and see what the water situation was over there. I came

inside, loaded all the empty water jugs (in case I got lucky), carried them out to the car and left it idling to warm up. Buddy was frantic with knowing he was going to get his "run." I locked the house, climbed in the car, and Buddy proudly paraded in front of me as we began the four-mile trek to the cabins at the creek.

As soon as I got to the top of the hill, my spirits lifted. The sight was magical. All the surrounding mountains were sprinkled with snow, looking like someone had spilled powdered sugar all over them. The frozen particles of ice glistened like quartz on a full sunny day. It was beautiful, stunning. I thought about all the other Christmas Days I'd had. It seemed like every Christmas, no matter how unlikely, some little miracle would happen. Maybe miracles happen every day and I just looked for them on Christmas Day. But this was the first year I was really conscious of actually expecting my Christmas miracle. And here it was in all its glory.

I probably took almost 45 minutes to drive the four miles to the creek, craning my neck like a tourist. And then, to a shriek of pure delight, I found the water pipes unfrozen and water running freely. I filled all the jugs, loaded them into the car, and took off for home. It was just as beautiful on the way back.

I stopped at "Trey's Hill," just to talk to him for a while. Standing there looking at the majesty all around me, I couldn't help but feel gratitude for the life Trey had shared with me. He could have loved anyone, but he loved me. I thanked him and told him how much I appreciated all that he had given me. I felt glad for him that he was able to grow up here on this ranch, and become the wonderful person he became. I felt like a queen, and that's what he had always called me, "My queen." I asked him to wait just a little longer for me, and he told my heart that he would. My second Christmas miracle of the season.

20

CHRISTMAS DAY

DAYBREAK WAS AGAIN GRAY AND dreary. Buddy was anxious to go out, so I jumped up and made coffee while he ran around outside. I had a sneaking feeling that I wouldn't be going into town this evening for my Christmas dinner with Renee and her family. The sky didn't look promising.

After checking the weather on the internet, I knew I'd have to stay home. It was supposed to have been in the high forties, but we weren't going to make it.

The new weather report said it wasn't going to be above freezing today, so I knew I'd have another day without water. I busied myself with mundane things . . . heating water I'd hauled from the cabins, answering the phone, checking email. My friend and go-to maintenance man, Dirk, called and said to open all the water faucets I could find to relieve the pressure if the temperature happened to get above freezing. I donned the same outfit: Trey's boots, camo jacket, gloves, and hiked around the property turning on faucets, making a mental map so I could retrace my steps and turn them off again should a miracle happen.

Then my father called, "just checking on you," he said. We talked about the presents he got for Christmas and it seemed his favorite was Michael Bublé's Christmas CD. He raved about it. As I listened to him struggle to try to describe the music, and try to remember who had sent it to him, I began to feel very sad, recognizing that I don't have that many more holidays to spend with him, that he, too, is mortal after all. And then it happened, just like that. My third Christmas miracle.

The water began sputtering through all the faucets I had opened, then gushing out. It sounded like music. It was "only"water, but not having any for three days gives you a much more tangible sense of appreciation. I said good-bye to Dad and ran all over the property like a crazy woman, turning off faucets. This time I skipped the camo jacket, the gloves and the heavy boots. It was warming up, after all.

21

GETTING READY FOR THE NEW YEAR

FOLKS ARE COMING FOR THE New Year's festivities. I had decided to have a small party, to welcome in another year, and have friends and family know how much I appreciate them. I email Jim and Gayle and they are actually coming the 487 miles just to wish me a happier new year. By the time I'm through with the guest list, I have around 25 people coming to the gathering. Ever the planner, I start making lists.

Since I spent the Christmas holidays making candy, chex mix, and cookies, all of that is done. I plan menus. I buy champagne, wine, vodka and all the mixings. The big cabin is booked with three friends Bill, Dennis, and Wayne. My son, Noah, will stay in the new cabin, and two other friends in the guest room here in the main house.

Then the bad news begins to arrive. Dennis is ill with diverticulitis and he and Bill won't be coming after all. Eli and Wayne are still coming without them. Then others begin to call and email regrets that they can't come. I make adjustments in the lists.

Finally the day arrives when people begin to actually show up. It is so great to see my son, and he is in his element with both dirt bikes in the back of the truck. The girls arrive and are in heaven at the cabin. Mark and Clair return from Christmas with family out of town, and it is wonderful to hear their voices again. We go through the week, anticipating New Year's Eve, and then the call comes.

Dennis has had a stroke and is in the hospital. Everyone's mood immediately drops into that abyss that only a phone call like that can illicit. Noah is a wreck and very emotional. I am sick at heart from the fear of yet another loss. Bill puts the best face on everything and calls several times giving updates. Finally, Dennis begins to improve.

The next day Bill calls and says a wonderful room on the 8th floor of the hospital has opened up and they are moving to it, already dubbing it "the party suite." Thanks to the immediate and excellent medical care, Dennis is already improving. They send internet pictures of their view of the Corpus Christi bay and Dennis has written on a large blackboard, sending his love to us. Now we know he is on the road to recovery.

The next 48 hours are filled with friends, booze, laughter, tears, food, music, motorcycles, and memories. We actually stay up until after midnight, ringing in the New Year with television fireworks and more laughter.

New Year's Day we prepare our feast: pot roast, ham, cornbread, black-eyed peas, salad and champagne. We lift our glasses to a toast of friends and all good wishes for the New Year. And then I notice there is one extra glass on the table. I knew immediately it was Trey's glass. I had unconsciously set out and filled an extra glass. I poured a bit of it into each of our glasses and we made our best toast of the day: "To Trey and his huge heart of love and sharing!" With glasses raised It dawns on me with stab-bing recognition that I am now facing a brand-new year without him. I feel paralyzed.

22

LEAVING

IT IS THE SECOND DAY of the new year and everyone is leaving today. I wake up early and decide to make Noah and Wayne a sack lunch for the road. I know Jim and Gayle will be leaving early and so I make a big pot of coffee. I (finally) get to take a shower and get dressed.

It doesn't start to get light until around 7:30. I try to clean up the kitchen mess and . . . yep . . . no water. Ahhh . . . will this never end? Now something else is wrong with the system because it didn't freeze last night. I wait for light so I can go outside and check for the problem. It figures. Everyone leaves at the same time and I am again plunged into this nightmare by myself. I am going to have to fix that.

23

BACK TO REALITY

MY MOOD BEGINS SINKING AS I watch Noah and Wayne until their truck is out of sight. Now everyone has gone and I busy myself for the rest of the day by cleaning the kitchen, doing a bit of laundry, and straightening the shop.

I need a way to turn off my brain. The monkey-mind continues its non-stop chatter; should I stay, should I go, what if I did this, did that, have I considered this, there probably wouldn't be enough money to do that, on and on in an endless loop. I remember that is what Xanax is for; to stop the loop.

I am depressed, as I realize that while people are around me, laughing, telling jokes, being friends, needing me to cook or be there for them in some way, I am not caught in this endless loop. The moment they are gone, though, my mind is like a limp noodle, unable to prop itself up and completely devoid of any feeling of self-confidence, peace, joy or strength.

I begin to cry.

I try to make myself stop.

I can't.

24

JANUARY 5, 2012

TEN MONTHS. IT'S BEEN TEN months today since Trey died. Why does it still feel like it was just yesterday? It's not that it is ever present on my mind. No. It's not that kind of "just yesterday" feeling. It sneaks up on you. The day started out like I'd planned for it to. It started out kind of normal.

I got up early, dressed, and drove to Odessa to see an ear, nose, throat specialist. I assumed I still had a sinus infection. I still had the headache, my eyes still hurt, I still felt stuffy, and I coughed. I assumed the antibiotics I'd taken two weeks ago after being diagnosed with a sinus infection didn't work. Of course, in rural America, the diagnosis was done by a physician's assistant, not a "real" doctor.

I arrived in Odessa and found the office building. I waited the obligatory hour and a half, and was then ushered in by the doctor, himself. He did all kinds of tests, probed every orifice on my head, squirted foul tasting spray up my nose and into my throat. Then he started going over the medications I was taking.

Finally he told me that he found no indication of any infection.

That a class of drugs, called Ace inhibitors, had side effects that produced the symptoms I was having. Lisinopril, the blood pressure medication the physician's assistant had prescribed for me back in August, was in that class of drugs. He said he couldn't be sure without a CAT scan, but he didn't think I had a sinus infection. I begged off on the CAT, saying I was still paying bills from Trey's death. He then threw away that order, and wrote one for a much cheaper x-ray of my sinus cavities, that would, "do almost as well." I said it didn't matter because I probably wouldn't get that done either. I said I would take his word for it.

It only cost me $40.00 and a day off from the shop to drive to Odessa and back to find out what I have known for years. Since I had no insurance for 15 years, I made sure I stayed healthy enough to stay away from doctors. Once I started seeing a "doctor" in August I had been sick with one thing or another ever since. Hmmm . . . how had I let that connection slip my mind? I resolved to throw away the lisinopril as soon as I got home and never to take it again. The doctor had said not to do that, but instead to take another kind. I think not.

The good part about the day, was that it was warm, with no wind, and sunny and cloudless. The hour and a half drive back to Alpine was tranquil. Relieved that I wasn't sick (just stupid) my mind wandered to other topics. Like Trey. Like how much I miss him. Like how nice it would have been to have had him with me, just for company, and to hear him say, like he always did, "See? We're in great shape! We don't NEED insurance!" And then I realized that today is January 5 . . . exactly ten months since he died. And then it was so obvious. An easy drive on a beautiful day that should have been enjoyable, but had a hovering of unease about it. And although I didn't start out consciously thinking about missing Trey, the missing part was still there. Still there, just under the radar of dealing with it. Even when the pain is unacknowledged for just a few hours, the heart knows. The heart knows that today it has been ten incredibly sad, monstrously hard months. My mood plummets. I think that if it is going to be this tortuous, I don't want to do it anymore. I just don't want to do it.

25

MEANINGLESSNESS

A GRAY SUNDAY ARRIVES. IT'S supposed to snow this evening, and tomorrow. I plan on how to get ready for it. Go to the cabins and turn on some water. Go into town and buy some basic supplies and mail bills in case the mail runs on Monday ("Neither rain, nor snow nor dark of night" doesn't always apply). I do a bit of laundry to kill some time until my rv renters tell me whether or not they'll stay another night. Then I settle in for the cold snap.

We get arctic air, but no snow here at the ranch. Still, I'm housebound due to ice on Big Hill . . . my one access into Alpine. I busy myself with doing laundry, anything to use water and keep it running. But by 4:00, the pipes are frozen anyway.

Tuesday dawns and at least we have sunshine. It warms up to around 50 degrees, but still I have no water. My guess is that now something besides frozen pipes is the reason. Now I have something else to worry about.

The 8:00 morning radio show comes on and announces that our one nursing home will close in 30 days. Many of the residents have been there for years. Many have no family left. It seems the politicos will again balance the budget on the backs of the elderly and children, while they stuff their pockets, take lavish vacations, grant themselves raises. "And the band played on."

I am in one of the darkest periods I have seen yet in this process. I miss Trey so much, and I miss LIFE. I miss just having the feeling that my physical, emotional, spiritual LIFE matters. It feels like nothing matters. And really, what DOES matter? I mean, ever? Do we all just live in this illusion that our jobs, our loves, our kids, our families, our squabbles, our hatreds somehow MATTER? During the course of our lives, when we retire from jobs, our loves die or leave, our kids grow up, our squabbles change and our hatreds find new outlets, what really matters?

I am feeling so bereft that I scare myself. I am having really bad thoughts. I can't quit crying. I go on these jags for days, until I am interrupted by some friend calling or it is time to pull myself together and open my shop for three days. Then it's back to silence and the dark.

A friend sends me an email of some quote for the new year and a website. I go to the website. The woman is a counselor, a healer, and an astrologer. I called her today and signed up for four counseling sessions, starting tomorrow night. I feel like a fool. I AM a counselor by profession and I can't even help myself. I feel ashamed to reach out. Why isn't it ok for me to ask for help? I will meditate on that.

26

THE DARK GETS DARKER

WEDNESDAY ARRIVES BRIGHT AND SUNNY, for a change. I have everything packed and ready to go into town as soon as my 10:00 telephone conference with the Farm Service Agency is completed. I have an appointment to have my hair cut, which always gives me a lift. I am going to water aerobics and hopefully the exercise will increase the endorphins or whatever-the-hell in my brain so I can break out of this funk.

I go out to the water pump and listen for signs of life. Nothing. Now I am getting an inkling of what is wrong. The pump is burned up. If that is the case, "only" $1,000 ought to take care of it. That, and a week or three for the well service people to get around to me.

So, again, I'm not going to have water any time soon.

27

THE DEEP GETS DEEPER

I SPOKE WITH THE COUNSELOR I found online last night. Primarily I just gave her a synopsis of what is going on in my world. She suggested visioning the way I want the sale of the ranch to go and then gave me some websites to go to that will connect me with others, somewhat alleviating my isolation. As soon as I got off the phone I went to the sites, and even joined one, although I didn't like the way you had to join. You had to give your real name, and after I went into the site people had their pictures posted. I think that's weird. There you are, out there for the world to see, or at least all the other members of the group whom you don't know, and have no idea what kind of people they are. Anyway, it was for free, and there are phone calls every Monday through Thursday on different topics: body, mind and soul. The first call is today and I'll probably get to it.

By some miracle the water well service people arrived this morning. The bottom line is the pump and motor are broken, the electronics (installed in May of last year) are shot, and the well has sand in it that needs to be dredged out. God only knows how much money this will cost. Yet more money dumped into this screwed up ranch. Another cold spell hits, and still, of course, no water until at least this evening.

I'm sick of everything. Even sick of myself. It's not that I WANT to die, it's that I want my life to stop being so painful and sad. I know how to make it stop. I have tons of pills and tons of guns. Why do I have to work so hard to make my life bearable? And what, really, is the point? Work like a jackass now so that in a few short years I can die a "natural" death? I think this ranch is haunted and jinxed. Look at how many lives it's claimed. Today, I don't mind being next, if it makes the pain stop. Screw this shit. Maybe if I say I hate my life long enough, God will just kill me. A new-age "suicide-by-cop" strategy.

28

THE MIDDLE OF JANUARY

IT DAWNED ON ME TODAY that this is already the middle of a new month. The first January without Trey. Another first. Yippee. At least today is sunny, if still cold. I finally have water again so at least that burden is lifted. I still have no idea what I'll have to pay for getting it fixed. It doesn't matter, I have water.

I decided today, after not hearing from the deer hunters, to cancel their lease and find a new group of guys, for a higher price. I feel as if they have taken advantage of me all last year, and have even violated their lease several times. They always say, "But we're friends, right?" Today I feel strong enough to know they are not my friends, just business associates who, really, have none of my interests at heart, only their own. That's the way business associates operate. It has nothing to do with friendship. And, while I'm on the topic, I start thinking about all the "friends" who appear, willy-nilly, when they need something from me. I'm going to do some work on removing myself from the circle of people who position themselves around me for personal gain. In a way, I've already begun that process just by identifying the phenomenon. The trick to determining who these people are, is to not need anything from them . . . to fix any and all of my own "neediness." I can do that.

And so the search for new deer hunters is underway. I emailed the first prospect, but of course he's dawdling with a million questions, and wants to come out, and blah the blah blah blah. I'll move on to the stack of other interested parties I have in my file. You snooze, you lose. I'm tired of waiting on everyone else. Maybe I'm just angry. I decide I'm turning into a bitch.

29

JANUARY 14

THE START OF A NEW year usually brings memories of all the old ones. Nostalgic review of past years has always been my start to begin anew.

But this January 14th I was swamped with customers. After such a long dry spell without making any money, I worked furiously in the shop. And to top it off, the recycle metal man came to remove some of the hideous junk around the house. And on top of THAT, my young friends from Lubbock came to do some work around the ranch in exchange for staying two nights in the big cabin. All of that necessitated me finding tools and wire for them to work with, and walking around the property pointing out to the metal man which piles of metal should be removed. In-between all of that, I waited on customers. I felt irritated and in a bad mood all day. I berated myself for hating everything no matter how it was. If there were no customers, I hated it. If there were too many customers, I hated it. If no one stopped by I was lonely and sad. If several stopped by, I was overwhelmed. Nothing was "right."

Sometime around one o'clock I finally had a minute to make

a sandwich. And of course, long-time ranch visitors (not quite friends) arrived. I had taken one bite. They visited for an hour or so, until more customers started coming. I forgot about lunch.

By 5:30 all the tourists had left and my daily books were done. I locked up the shop and headed down to my office to post receipts, and then suddenly burst into tears. "This is January 14!" Oh DAMNIT, another first. How could I have forgotten about it all day? How could I have gone all day without knowing it? It was/ would have been our 11th anniversary. And I would spend it, of course, without Trey.

Through the fog of tears, I thought back on the plans we had made to get married. I remember we were tired of trying to make all the wedding arrangements. Relatives we could barely tolerate were planning on coming and staying with us for weeks . . . just what a newly married couple wants. It was also getting expensive. Different ones needed to be picked up at the Midland airport and brought to the ranch. Then there would be the inevitable problem of getting them to and from town. It was all exhausting. 9/11 had just happened and we had a new awareness of how tentative things in life can be. We just wanted to get married.

It seemed so much easier to just go to our friend, the Justice of the Peace, and stand in his office, and say the magic words. Perfect. And so, on January 14, 2002 we were married. Even if you've been living together for years, even if you've waited for even more years than that, getting married is an event. We were nervous. We dressed up in our "finery," Trey in black jeans, white shirt, and black leather vest, me in my gray and white sweater dress and my best boots. We came home and called friends and relatives and told them it was done, and the next day we left for a short honeymoon. I laughed saying we could never forget our anniversary since it was exactly one month before Valentine's Day. Trey, never one for remembering dates and looking dubious, replied, "Valentine's Day?"

The god-awful, staggering sadness of it all just dropped me to my knees, and I couldn't stop crying. I sat on those steps to the warehouse, surrounded by the left-over pieces of the ill-timed garage sale (things still not put away), the generations of inventory in various stages of change, the old cliff sparrows' nests in the rafters, and the fading sunlight. I cried for what could have been, for what should have been. I cried for the loneliness. I cried because, looking back, this had been such a wonderful day, eleven years ago. I cried because Trey is gone and I can't be with him. I cried because we would make little silly home-made anniversary cards. One year, he drew mine on a paper plate. I still have them . . . somewhere.

Finally the grief/guilt attack subsided. I went to my office, posted my books, took a shower, and left for my friend's son's 17th birthday party, amazed (again) that little pieces of life have to go on. I am amazed that I am tasked with weaving it all together. Weaving it into some strange tapestry that, in the end, will not matter to anyone.

30

LIFE GOES ON

THE LITTLE BIRTHDAY PARTY WAS not fun. For some reason Clair was in a bad mood, and Mark was doing his best to cover up her remarks. It was uncomfortable. I spent most of the time eating my pizza, and discussing college plans with their son, the birthday boy.

When I am with couples now, I see how easily we all take each other for granted, believing that "the road goes on forever and the party never ends." What does it matter that I say something to my husband I would never say to just a friend? What does it matter that I act as if the world revolves only around me? There's always tomorrow to make up, to apologize, to vow to ourselves we will do better. Rarely do we prostrate ourselves before the one we have offended in a true offering of regret and apology. Rarely do we actually name the offense we gave, and rarely do we honestly ask for forgiveness. And it is when death intervenes that we remember those horrible statements, those shooting-dagger looks, those annoyed and heavy sighs. Only then do we suffer what we have dealt.

The next day Mark and Clair were supposed to come out to the ranch for lunch. I received a phone call from David, the Birthday Boy, that they had had an accident about 4 miles outside of town. I turned off the stove and raced to the accident site. Mark was pinned in the car. His younger son, Bowie, was in the ambulance, almost hysterical with pain. His daughter was dazed but unhurt. Clair had not been with them. The car was a total wreck.

The next 8 hours or so I spent in the emergency room, helping Clair to see about getting David and Bowie air lifted to Odessa, and trying to keep their daughter calm. From time to time Mark was screaming, I could hear Bowie crying, and Clair and the small hospital staff were rushing around in some horrible dance of trauma.

It was the first time I had been back at the hospital since the day Trey had died. Even the same nurses were in the emergency room. I was having flashbacks. I was trying to stay calm and be present in the moment, but different voices kept coming back in my memories. "We need to transport him."

"No. He's decided to stay here. We won't go."

"We don't have an I.C.U."

"I don't care. Trey wants to be here with his friends and family."

"But there's nothing we can do for him here, except make him comfortable. If we send him to Odessa he could have another few days, possibly a week."

The voices in my head contrasted with the voices in the hall. This time, Clair was pleading to have her husband transported. This time, there was hope.

By 9:00 pm Clair was leaving in a borrowed car with Bowie to drive to Odessa. Mark had already been transported by plane. I walked through the dark parking lot and found my car.

Driving back to the ranch was surreal. In my mind, it was March 5 and Trey had just died. I thought about going home to an empty house. I thought about all the things I wished I had said, and all the things I was sorry that I did say. I thought about how life is like a material woven of every emotion available in the realm of human experience. I cried and told Trey out loud how sorry I was that I had not been able to save him. I cried and told myself that I wished it had been me instead of him. And then I got home, and just cried.

31

DEFAULT MODE

I HAD AN AMAZING DREAM. I was following Trey around outside and he was always just a few feet ahead of me, and turning a corner. I tried and tried to catch up to him. I could only see the back of his figure, and just barely as he escaped around yet another turn. Finally, I was in the front yard, and he had just turned into the house. As I continued walking towards the house I had to walk under the mulberry tree in the front yard. Directly underneath it, I looked up. There in the branches was a tiger, his eyes gleaming red in the gathering twilight. I stood stock still, transfixed. And then he pounced. He jumped directly onto me and began eating me. I woke up.

It was a disturbing dream on many levels, and so I began an internet search of the symbolism of the tiger. Strength, fear, power, were the memorable words that came up. I recognized that I was, indeed, fearful of what the next chapter in my life would be. Once the ranch is sold, who will I be? Once I'm relieved of all the hard work of ranch life, what will I do? I decided to start trying to answer those questions, to start to think of a plan for what is to come after the ranch is gone from me. I mean, it's not like I haven't been thinking and trying to plan. Months ago when I finally reached the decision to begin the process of selling the ranch, I tried to think of a place I would like to be once the property is sold. I've had very little results, always finding a reason that one place or another wouldn't work, discarding one idea after another, and moving on to a new scenario.

A few nights later I had another dream. I was at Clair's house at Easter. Bowie and I were dying Easter eggs. The ones that Bowie was making were vivid hues of every color, each one more beautiful that the last. My eggs, however, would not hold the dye. No matter how long I left them in the cup of dye, they came out white.

After I woke up, I thought about that dream. Easter and the Resurrection. Eggs and the beginning of life. Appropriate, I thought. After death by tiger, a resurrection into a new world, a new way of being, a new life. I became more aware of how our subconscious works on our problems while we are asleep, while we are unconscious. This was not a new realization, but it certainly was one with a deeper sense of meaning than I'd ever had.

Working through the symbolism and meanings of the dreams, I came to realize that I have been saying for years now that, "I am so tired." I'm tired of always having to be the strong one. I'm tired of always having to be the one who takes the lead. I'm tired of my relationships being built on the premise that I will "fix" someone or take the lead. I looked back in journals I had kept in the 70's and 80's. Even then, 40 years ago, I was recognizing that I didn't want to always have to be the "strong" one! Now, why is that? If I'm really "so tired," why do I continue to be the one who can fix things? What payoff do I get for being "the strong one?"

"Well," I thought, "I get to be in control. I get to be the one that others have to trust. I don't have to trust anyone else. I am fully competent, so why should I place trust in someone else who might not be?" And that thought was like hitting bedrock. I have trouble trusting. I have trouble trusting people, airplanes, automobiles, new situations, restaurants, bridges, doctors. As I silently thought about all the things I don't trust, I began to see how long the list was, and how long I had been building that list. Starting in very early childhood I learned that it was dangerous to trust. I learned how to be competent. No trust would inevitably equal no disappointment. About that time I figured out that I was the only thing I *could* trust.

I had used the unconscious "don't trust anybody or anything" belief as my automatic default mode of behavior. No wonder I was tired! I couldn't even remember when the last time I did trust someone had occurred. Without trusting, I never had to be disappointed. Sooner or later the object of my trust would fail to hit the mark, and thus disappointment would be the end.

No trust also meant no support. I could not allow myself to feel support because that would mean I had let down my guard . . . I had allowed someone else to do my job.

I suppose I could have delved deeper into even more understanding of this syndrome, but I had seen too much already. I decided to "bring my dreams to life," as a way of understanding myself more.

And so the next morning, I cut out paper egg shapes and painted them vibrant colors. I marked each one with a word that symbolized what I would like my "resurrected" life to look like and feel like. I wrote words like "supported," "fun," "relaxing," "financially stable," "spiritually stable," and "soft." Like the Sears ad, I wanted to birth a softer side of me. A side that didn't resort to my default mode of distrust. A side that allowed others to support me. A side that gave me a bit of time to become someone else and begin anew. A side that enabled me to become more than I was.

I decided to bring the message of the tiger to life, too. I made prayer flags from the leftover pieces of my cutout eggs and painted words representing the characteristics I would need to birth my new life. I wrote "self-confidence," "courage," "power," and "vitality." I hung the prayer flags outside on the tiger tree. I felt happier than I had in a long, long time.

32

A NEW MONTH

THAT HAPPY FEELING LASTED EXACTLY 3.5 days. Life encroached again and worries about Mark and Clair, their children, the ranch, the chain across the road to the cabins, the deer hunters, the taxes, the taxes unpaid, the bill for the new well and pump, and a million other things began to consume my time again. And so February began.

Another "first." This Valentine's Day will be different. I decide not to dwell on it until later. I can't foretell the future, so who knows what that sweet day will actually be like until it gets here? The whole of February looms in front of me, and already business is picking up to the point I can just barely squeeze everything in. The public is demanding. Even when I tell them I am closed Sunday through Wednesday, they figure out a way to make me work. They are smarter than I am I suppose.

And beyond the work schedule, I am still consumed with all the minutiae of the ranch. This place is such a burden . . . a beautiful burden. I keep reminding myself that I should be enjoying it, before it is gone . . . and that may be soon. In Odessa on Monday a friend introduced me to a man who is interested in buying the ranch and who will come out soon to look it over. He has enough money to pull the price out of his back pocket I was told. Now all that is left is to get my brother-in-law, Donald, on board with the sale of the ranch.

33

YESTERDAY, TODAY AND TOMORROW

I TRY NOT TO LIVE all three days at once. But it has occurred to me that it is almost impossible not to. My everyday "today" is filled with things I have to do, lists to make, trips to town to take, customers to acquiesce to, animals to feed, clothes to wash and all the other mundane chores of life. And then there's "yesterday." Did I remember to turn off the heaters in the shop? Did I forget to charge that couple for the one item they bought in the shop? Did I make those phone calls to get that information? And crowded on top of all of that, "tomorrow" waits. Did I finish that list of what to do when I get to town? Did I do the accounting to take to the CPA? Have I gathered up all the important papers to take to the tax office? It seems that every day begins with checking my calendar. Things are so crowded I even have to make appointments for phone calls with friends. It's all a dizzying dance of "shoulds," "musts," and "maybes."

I thought of the image of a beautiful merry-go-round. The painted horses are going up and down, the music is tinkling unceasingly, and the whole carousel is constantly going around and around and around in a blur of lights, sounds and colors. At the edge of the carousel the centrifugal force pulls me in ever faster directions, first up, then down, all the while whirling around on its giddy orbit. But, moving to the center of the carousel, I am more grounded, less in the midst of all the activity, and able to be quiet and outside the forces that pull in all directions.

Living in "yesterday," brings either remorse or satisfaction, depending on the judgment I cast upon myself. Living in "tomorrow," brings either anxiety or hopeful anticipation. Living in "today," brings me into the center of the carousel and gives me the ability to have focused concentration.

34

VULNERABILITY

I LEARNED A GREAT LESSON about myself today. I learned that when my heart goes out to someone in sympathy or empathy, I feel a huge desire to "help" that person. I jump right into my "fixit" mentality. Like the old Mighty Mouse song, "Here I come to save the day! Mighty Mouse is on the way . . ." Of course, it's my old default behavior. That, coupled with my southern upbringing that mandates all females be "nice" all the time, my vulnerability could be dangerous.

I need a danger alarm. I need a way to "see through" the lies and projections that people use to manipulate me. I need to learn to be doubtful. I need to adopt the attitude that you have to earn my trust, and that it is not given away freely even when you tell me the most heart-wrenching story I've ever heard. My own stories are heart-wrenching enough.

35

FEBRUARY COLD

I AM FAIRLY SHRINKING FROM the cold depth of winter. Living in a rock house is like living in a cave. Once the cold sets in, it will not warm up no matter how much heat you poor into it. Even with leaving the water in the bath tub running at night, the pipes freeze. Usually I have water by 10:00 am again the next morning. The cold, and the gray, and the wind combine to paralyze me in the same old thoughts. I feel encased in some dark cast that just will not break apart. Sometimes it feels like anesthesia, like my eyes are open but my brain does not process any input. Surely spring is on the way?

36

VALENTINE'S DAY

THE PHONE RINGS AT 7:00 am. I had decided to sleep "late" today, as a Valentine's Day gift to myself. I got up to answer the phone, let the dog out, and feed the cat. The caller was an old friend who had been to the ranch several times. Trey and I used to sit up late with him and his wife and play cards, after their day of hiking. He is bringing his grown sons out this weekend to visit. We talked for a few minutes and then he mentioned his youngest son had died last week. His voice sounded like he was just reporting the temperature, like a common occurrence had just happened. It was so nonchalant I almost said, "You're kidding!" but managed to stop myself in mid-sentence. I followed his lead and kept my voice level and unsurprised. When we had finished our conversation, I stood, stunned, with the phone in my hand. Last WEEK? And he can talk? Last week, and he can laugh and carry on a conversation? I am astounded. What is wrong with me? Eleven months after Trey's death and I still cry every chance I get. I still have thoughts peppered with his voice, his sayings, his vision, his dreams for the ranch. I feel on the verge of nausea every day. I feel lost, and alone, and crazy. I feel like I want to go to bed and never get up.

But the phone rings again. This time the buyer for the water tanks is coming to pick them up today, "If it's all right." Now there's a phrase for you. "All right." Semantics have taken on a new meaning. No, nothing is "right" much less ALL is right, but, yeah, come pick up the tanks. I need the $500.00. Of course, I don't tell him that. I act normal. Natural. I act like I'm a stable person, not like a person who's ready to slit her own throat if only I had the courage. "Of course," I say in my most casual voice, "I'll see you in about an hour." The call had stopped what promised to be a deluge of tears. Maybe that's what my friend was doing. Maybe by acting "normal" we keep at bay the awful realization that part of you is missing. Maybe, we can stay in denial long enough to get our day done.

The second call of the day and it's not even 9:00 yet. I suppose I could take these calls as signs. Signs that today will be unusual. Signs that tell me anything can happen today. Signs that say I really shouldn't plan too much, but rather let the day flow as it will. I take a quick shower and put on my most un-valentine-like outfit. I just want it to be over. I just want it to be night, and sit in front of the television, and eat the box of chocolate candies I bought for myself for Valentine's Day.

37

UNEXPECTED GUESTS

As usual, everything was happening all at once. The phone was ringing and a huge motorhome had just parked in the rv park. I was on my way to the shop to open for the day, and my "ranch hand" had just arrived. By the time I walked out to greet the motorhome folks, they were walking to my door with a beautiful bouquet of yellow and red roses, crying. Friends of the ranch for many years, they had just been told in town of Trey's death.

It is so hard to help Trey's friends through the early stages of grief when I am not even able to help myself. It is always such a touching tribute to Trey to see just how many people had come to love and respect him. At the same time, it is a heavy burden to answer the inevitable questions of how? When? Why?

We talked and cried for a while, and then my day began to accelerate. Customers were arriving, the worker needed direction, the phone was still ringing. I invited them for drinks later that evening.

The day wore on, but I was never quite able to pull myself out of the early morning grieving. I felt on the verge of tears for the rest of the day, and finally closed the shop, exhausted. Then I prepared for the evening talk I had promised. We talked until late in the evening, and after they left I still had a phone call promised to a girlfriend. More talking, more analyzing, more processing, as only girlfriends can. I went to bed around midnight, beyond tired.

At 7 am the phone rang. As I tried to reach the phone before voicemail clicked in, I noticed a car parked in the driveway. Customers waiting for me. Telephone ringing. It was beginning to feel like a replay of the day before. I decided to ignore both the phone and the customers, start my coffee and take a shower. That decision alone made me feel better.

The work of the day continued until around 5 pm when my attorney called, letting me know she advised me to try once again to talk to Trey's brother, Donald, about the ranch finances and its necessary sale. Trey's brother was obviously in denial about the dire straits the finances of the ranch were coming to, unaware of the process needed to be able to save something for his children and the grandchildren, delusional about how the ranch was run, and completely unable to understand the legal ramifications of all of it.

In lieu of completely falling apart, I poured myself a drink and sat thinking about all the "new age," "alternative," ways to look at this development. "Everything happens for a reason," it is said. "You can't push the river," bubbles up from some forgotten sage. "God does everything right on time," my Baptist memories relay. The truth is, I am boiling with exhaustion and yet back to square one, facing more, lengthy, costly dealings with a brother-in-law who seems indifferent. It's like beginning another race, worn out from the one you just completed. I need for something concrete to happen with this ranch before I am completely penniless and unable to affect what needs to happen. I am running out of ideas, and running out of energy. I don't know what to do next. I don't know who to call, and if I did I wouldn't know what to say. I decide to take a Xanax and go to bed.

38

LAST LOOKS

ANOTHER BOOK BEGINS TO FORM in my mind. It will take the shape of vignettes about the last time you saw something, or heard something, that turned out to be a meaningful, fork-in-the-road kind of moment. When you lose something, it is a joke that sometimes well-meaning helpers ask, "Where did you lose it?" If you knew, of course it wouldn't be lost. If you knew something was happening for the last time, or that you were hearing or seeing something for the last time, you would probably take better note, or, perhaps, do something, anything, to ensure that, indeed, it wasn't the last time.

I remember that when Trey and I returned from getting the awful news of his advanced cancer it was the kind of day one can never forget. The ranch was surrounded by fires on almost every side; Hawkins ranch to the west, Yarbrough Ranch to the south, and smaller fires everywhere else. The air was filled with smoke from thousands of mesquite trees burning, and permeated everything with what smelled like a huge bar-b-que. Of course there were customers waiting for us when we returned from the doctor's office to the ranch that day. My voice, like my courage, had left me.

I struggled to find a way to speak and "carry on." Trey walked up and said, "I'm going to saddle Goldie and ride down to the creek to get the Longhorns. That fire may jump the creek and I don't want the cows down there." I immediately told him not to go, that the cows would be all right. I pleaded that I needed him to help me with the customers . . . a million arguments to keep him home and close to me. He smiled that easy smile he had and told me not to be "silly." "It will only take about 30 minutes," he said, "I'll be back in no time."

I watched him saddle the horse and swing himself up. The image was blurred because there were tears in my eyes. I had a queasy, nagging feeling in my gut. Something similar to panic welled up inside me, even as I explained it away as "just sorrow" from the diagnosis.

They took off through the pens and up the slope of the first hill. I couldn't take my eyes off him. Everything around me stood completely still, and even my hearing was suspended. I felt that this was a huge moment, but I didn't know it would be the last moment. I didn't know it would be the last time I would see him gently hold those reigns and amble Goldie so easily off to the horizon.

Sure enough, it was only about an hour before he returned with the Longhorns. He looked tired, but happy and in good spirits. We invited his sister, Beverly, and her husband over that evening. I didn't want to tell Beverly over the phone, so earlier I had called her husband and asked him to let her know the devastating diagnosis. Our evening get-together was to be happy, and a chance to visit before things got "really bad."

In my mind, I thought Trey probably had 3 to 6 months to live. Not as much as we would have liked, of course, but enough time to truly "live" our lives together, and to get ready for our final good-bye. That night we laughed and told stories of funny things from the past, and generally enjoyed our time together. Trey seemed light, somehow, jumping up to get water and things for people, and genuinely enjoying the evening. I was glad we had a respite from the heavy thoughts of cancer, of death.

The next day Trey was ill, "probably from a virus," he said. And the next day, he died.

Looking back on it now, I know Trey took that last ride because it was what he loved to do. He knew it would be the last, but I didn't. Or maybe he wanted to get the cows up to the pens so that it would be easier for me to feed them after he was gone. Maybe both.

And as the days of this year creep inexorably towards March 5, the day Trey died, I find myself remembering what we did on these last few and dwindling days a year ago. How, unknowing, we were edging ever closer to our final kiss, our last touch, the last hug, the last laugh. It's a deep, dark thing to know that if you had only seen the signs better, or been more aware, or more compassionate, or more loving, or more easy going, or a million more things that I wasn't, that I could have affected the outcome. I could have somehow, kept him here with me longer. I will forever cherish the last image of him riding toward the western sky, sitting easy in his saddle, his dog trotting alongside. Trey was a simple man, and I know, to him, he was already in heaven.

39

LEARNING PATIENCE

IT OCCURS TO ME THAT most of this year has been an opportunity to learn patience. Early on, learning how to have patience with friends who were just finding out about Trey's death, family members who wanted to "help," customers who didn't understand why I wasn't open when I said I would be, and a million other "teachable moments."

By the fall I had realized I had no way to continue to support the ranch. And so, more opportunities arose to try and show Trey's brother, and absentee part-owner, that we would have to sell the ranch. That on-going saga has been eye-opening in the realm of what happens to families when one member dies. Especially if the departed member owns a majority of the estate.

I have discovered that in many areas, the "law" is a sham. If you own part of an estate in UNDIVIDED SHARES, it is an open invitation for one or all parties to exercise their sense of power, control and entitlement. The "law" will not help you. The "law" exists only to make sure the lawyers, the county and the state unburden you of your undivided property, to their benefit. It is in no way fair to any stakeholder in the property.

And so here I am, the majority stakeholder, a 65-year-old widow, living alone on a very remote ranch, 20 miles from the nearest town, with a family of in-laws who will no longer even speak to me, trying to keep the ranch together for me, for them, and for our heirs.

I have run out of financial resources. Trey's brother, Donald, neglects paying for his share of the property taxes, their father's mortgage, or any expenses of the ranch. Even before Trey died, when we so desperately needed money for medical expenses, Donald was unwilling to help in any way. I tried reasoning with him all through last fall, emailing him, having an attorney write to him, and calling him, all to no avail.

I consider him to be not only ignorant of what is at stake, but also unable to understand even what is explained to him. Like his father before him, Donald is very much the procrastinator and it is hard for him to make even minimal choices. And, like his father, he seems to be somewhat of a hoarder, and his home is cluttered with the debris of decades. There is a small and narrowing path that winds throughout his home. It is the same state the ranch was in when I arrived to help Trey.

Even though I am a certified counselor, I have never been able to understand the process that causes hoarding. Of course, on a spiritual level, it is fear that underlies such a terrible, diminishing condition. One operates out of fear, or out of love. When fear is in charge, no amount of talking, bargaining, or compromising will have any effect to the good of all, or even to the good of the individual so afflicted. Perhaps that is all that procrastination is. Putting off decisions is like keeping everything still around you, hoarding the way things "are" if you will. Donald is a smart man, but somehow he doesn't see that making no decision is still a decision . . . it will have consequences. And in this case, the consequence will be losing the ranch. I cannot keep it afloat by myself much longer. Ever the optimist, though, I have made one last good faith effort to contact Donald. I called and left a message on his voice mail to please call. That was a week ago and I have heard nothing. Reality is a harsh mistress.

40

MARCH 5, AGAIN

I TRIED TO MAKE PLANS for this first anniversary of Trey's death. My big plan included not answering the phone, locking the gate to the ranch, lighting candles, staying in the hot tub as much as possible, and, at sunset, taking the little stone that is engraved with "Let your heart rest here," to the hill where Trey's ashes were sprinkled. Several of my very best friends sent emails, letting me know they are remembering this day with me, and that is a blessing I will never forget. That is the extent of my plan. I don't trust myself to be around people, knowing that I can burst into tears for any reason or for no reason.

There is no way to understand this death thing. No way to reason through it. No way to deny it. All you can do is feel it. And in that sense it is a living thing. Something never to be forgotten or left behind. Something ever present. I don't know how I got through most of my life without knowing this. But once you know, you can't un-know.

Among my peers I am early at this spousal death thing. Maybe when my friends are facing this issue I will be of some help to them. Or maybe this will just teach me how to be there for them when the time comes. For it is surely coming, and, even now, they don't consciously know it is "down the road," lurking like some ambush of the emotions, waiting to destroy everything they thought they knew.

41

AGREEMENT (At last)

I WAS FINALLY ABLE TO reach my brother-in-law. I told Donald that I knew he was concerned about the family heirlooms and the museum quality inventory in the shop. I told him they were his. I told him that all I wanted was Trey's saddle and gun. Everything else would be for him to keep or otherwise dispose of. There was a long silence. When he spoke, I could hear the tears in his voice.

I had always assumed that he and most of the rest of the family had demonized me to the point where they were thinking that I only wanted to pillage the family of everything and sell the ranch. Sometimes I thought I could hear them in my mind, calling me names and painting me with the "ugly sister-in-law" stereotypes. So now, when the truth came out, he was almost speechless.

I told him then that I had been unable to pay the property taxes for the previous year because I had had to re-do the well here at the house and buy a new pump. Further, I told him I would be unable to pay the last mortgage note on the ranch (encumbrances from his father, his sister Beverly, and him) due July first. I told him we needed to sell the ranch, and sell as fast as possible. And then, as

I had suspected, he stated that since the ranch "wasn't worth very much" he did not want to sell. I asked him what he meant. "Well, according to the property tax assessments, the value is not very much," he said, in his most assertive voice, as if he had been duly noting all paperwork for the last twelve years.

So that was it. He had thought all along the value of the ranch was the assessed value on the tax statements! He had no idea what the market value was.

I told him I wasn't sure of the market value, but that from what I had seen other ranches in the area bring, I thought it would be worth much, much more. I said, "Even using a conservative estimate it would still be enough to pay off ranch debt and have some left over for the kids and grandkids." There was complete silence. I went on, "Or we could just sit here and let it deteriorate since neither one of us has the money to keep it up. Last year the old storage house blew apart in a small tornado. This year, your grandfather's garage completely gave way and caved in. I can just about guarantee you the next problem will be the roof on the house. So, it's up to you. What do you want to do?" He said quietly, "I'll talk to my wife and get back to you tomorrow."

42

THE DECISION IS MADE

THE FOLLOWING DAY I WAITED for my Donald's call, but heard nothing. Then, the evening of the next day, he called and simply said, "Let's sell." I invited him to come to the ranch the following weekend so we could settle "small details."

The following weekend he arrived with wife and grandson in tow. It had been so many years since he had actually spent any time on the ranch, and had not realized the magnitude of the number of heirlooms collected throughout the generations. He was quite overcome with amazement.

I wasn't surprised that the weekend went so well, but I was enormously grateful for the congeniality and closeness we all seemed to feel. I was also overcome with the sense of relief I felt in having the burden of the ranch lifted from my shoulders alone. It was so great I felt . . . almost . . . happy.

43

THE SECOND YEAR BEGINS

IT IS MARCH 27. EXACTLY one year and twenty two days since Tr . . . my fingers pause above the keyboard, not wanting to type the word, "died." I think I thought, somewhere in the recess of my not-right brain, that by now things would be easier. I didn't stop to reason it out or analyze it, I just thought that somehow after the first year it would be easier to get from day to day. I am surprised by the dull depression that has set in, bringing any activity to a crawl. When I do think about it, I think this is probably a blessing, especially at my age. At sixty-something time usually seems to fly by you, racing into some hectic last stage of living, leaving one frantic to complete the "bucket list" or at least to stop thinking about it. But now time has slowed to become an inch by inch companion.

Now I have time to clean the house, clean the patio, eat breakfast, make lunch, do the laundry, each endeavor completed and still it is only midday. Time seems to drag through a never-ending series of tasks, and, try as I may, they just don't seem to matter.

I think nothing will ever "matter" again. Just a stretch of time from now until I'm not here anymore, punctuated by small respites or large catastrophes both inconsequential in the face of death. My own, or someone else's. We all have a ticket to ride.

44

A TEST OF HEART

MORE DREAMS LAST NIGHT OF a tortuous kind. Trey's father, Frank, was in the shop with me and I was trying to help him with something. The shop was dark and dusty, the way it really was during Frank's tenure here at the ranch. He kept dithering around while I went through moldy box after moldy box to find the items I needed. The dim light made it hard to see. Other people were there, milling about, wanting to buy merchandise and the whole shop was crowded and uncomfortable.

The dog woke me up needing to go outside. After that chore, I went back to bed and thought about my dream. It was telling me that something would have to be done with all the inventory. What would I do with all of it? When should I start packing? What should I pack things in? Where would I put things? These questions led to, not only an increased heart rate, but a feeling that time was running out. A feeling that I had best be here today and start the job. A feeling so opposite from yesterday's slow meandering through the day that I was caught off guard.

I had one arranged chore to do today . . . a hair appointment.

Thank God. That would make me feel better. That would be a bit of luxury that would lift my spirits and make the rest of the day bearable.

I checked my email before showering and getting ready for the appointment. I stared at the message from my sister-in-law. "I can't sleep. I have many questions. Like, is there a timeline for selling the ranch? Are you leaving?"

How bizarre. I stared at the message and re-read it several times. I thought about Church last Sunday and how the lesson was Psalm 1: "Don't walk with the wicked, stand with the sinners, or sit with the mockers." Is this coincidental that the message comes the very day after I emailed her brother asking him what he wanted to do about hiring an appraiser for the ranch? Word travels fast, but it would have been fine if she had just called me, or stayed in touch with me. I suppose we do what we can do, and sometimes even that is hard.

I debate what to do. Answer the email? Be alarmed? I decide to put myself in her place. WHY would she be asking me these questions? Does she want to visit the ranch before it is sold? Maybe several times? Does she think she can come and pick out items from the shop? Is she just sad that she is now out of the loop regarding any business of the ranch? Does she regret putting herself out of the loop? The answer to the last question I am quite sure is, "yes."

After praying about the situation, I decide to call her and invite her to lunch. I call and she is surprised and quite happy that I did. I hear in her voice a huge relief of some kind. We will see what this brings.

45

EVERY DAY IS A SURPRISE

As I FINISHED GETTING DRESSED to go to the hair appointment, I managed to twist my back the wrong way. I felt it immediately. A stabbing, pulsating pain in my lower left back. I decided to try and ignore it, to "walk it off." I rushed out to my appointment.

Arriving early, my beautician was in a meeting with two other women. All of them spoke rapidly in Spanish and I couldn't understand a word, so I took a seat in the back and waited, berating myself for hurrying to an appointment that was obviously no big deal to anyone but me.

Lunchtime arrived and my sister-in-law and I began a chit-chat type of conversation. As the meal wore on we both apologized for our miscommunications and misdeeds, without going much into detail. I kept wondering what she wanted. I didn't have a clue what she was wondering.

We didn't get a lot "solved," but I think we both left feeling like some of the ice had been broken. She related how her father had refused to give her and her then husband the ranch. Then he allowed as to how he would give her husband the ranch, but not her. She was clearly still hurt by the insult of so many years ago, even knowing that her father was egotistical, narcissistic, and a woman-hater to boot. We both laughed when she said, "I guess he's rolling in his grave knowing a woman inherited MOST of the ranch!" It was something we could both agree on.

By now my back was screaming for help, and so we ended lunch, said our good-byes and left. I went to the chiropractor for an adjustment and came home as fast as I could, heading straight for the hot tub.

And then the phone rang and it was again my sister-in-law, inquiring as to the condition of my back. I thanked her properly for lunch (she had insisted on paying) and she said she had written two emails, remembering how the miscommunication had happened in the first place. We said no more about it, but when I read the emails it seemed to me to be another complete re-write of history, with even the wrong dates. A twist to make me wrong (again) and her right. I started to get that gut feeling again. Something just wasn't right.

And then, lo and behold, the very next day was an email from one of Trey's cousins. The one who didn't come to his memorial. The one who had not called out of concern for me or for the ranch for an entire year. The one who had never said a word to me through all the hell of the previous year. It was a message from facebook wanting to be "friends."

All of this sudden family contact is pure coincidence, I said to myself. Just because a proposed value of the ranch has been talked about for two weeks, via the brother-in-law, family members would not be so crass as to start crawling out of the woodwork. Surely I am a conniving bitch to even think such a thing. Surely they are contacting me to be real, true friends, who really, truly care about me, even though I have not heard from them in over a year.

It is disorienting in so many ways to lose the one person you have come to trust implicitly. Who is your friend? Who is your foe? Are there any foes? Who is manipulating you? Who is loyal? Who is safe? Should I depend on my brain to know, or my gut?

I suppose only time will tell. In a family, when one member dies, everyone loses someone . . . a spouse, a brother, a father, an uncle. It is not an easy thing to get through the loss, much less find the grace to overlook old hurts, old feuds. Death . . . the great teacher.

46

IT FEELS LIKE A RESURRECTION

Easter is approaching and so many new feelings are surfacing. Even the weather is milder and the horrid wind has slowed on most days now. I feel a new feeling of some sort of resolution arising. Today I called an appraiser for the ranch and hired him. He will begin in about two weeks, and should be through by the first week or so in May. And so, the sale of the ranch is becoming more and more real to me. Instead of the anxiety I experienced just last fall at the very thought of selling my home, now I feel a sense of coming completion. It is a comfort to know that I can still visit "Trey's Hill" any time I want, as it is right off a county road. But it is still an empty feeling to think that my road with Trey, in a sense, is ending. Not being with him on the ranch still seems unbelievable.

We first met in 1977, when his parents hired me to help his mother in the house, and his father in the rock shop. I was ecstatic. It was like "Little House on the Prairie," or "The Waltons." There was a huge garden, milk cow, fruit trees, ranch hands, and lots of customers and tourists. That meant vegetables and fruit to can and preserve, family, workers and customers to cook for, and a thousand other chores that I loved doing. Trey's job was to work the cows and take care of the horses. There was no television reception, no radio except for an am station from Alpine, and so our evenings were filled with sitting on the porch of Trey's grandfather's house talking, laughing, playing cards, and falling in love. It was idyllic. It could have been a hundred years ago. I've always said, "Life is long, but fast."

47

EASTER

IT'S PRETTY CLEAR NOW, EVEN to me, that I'm panicking. I thought I could load one more holiday on top of everything else I'm doing. I thought I was like I used to be, before Trey died. I thought a family holiday would be do-able. I was wrong.

Trey's son from a previous marriage, Bobby, and his wife and their four children came to visit for Easter. All the children were under eight years old, the youngest a year and a half, and all of them running, bumping, jumping, crying, yelling, moving all the time. They arrived about midday on Saturday and we busied ourselves with coloring Easter eggs. After that it was a mad scramble to fix dinner and actually get the children to sit down and eat it. Okay, we didn't sit, they ate on the move. Somehow we got to the end of the evening and they left for the cabin. After cleaning up dinner, I made burritos for church on Sunday, the Easter sunrise service.

Sunday morning, 5:00 am arrived. Church was wonderful and moving (there's that word again.) We arrived home and I began to cook for the Easter dinner: turkey and dressing, pork ribs, mashed potatoes, salad and peach cobbler. I had done all the prep work so I thought it would be easy. It wasn't.

The children defied logic. The two dogs who accompanied the crew didn't help. The day wore on. Finally the family and other guests (yes, there were three other invited guests) were assembled. We said a quick blessing and ate. Then it was time to clean up again.

Thank God for helpful guests. I didn't have it all to do alone. But by the time it was over I was ready to pass out, literally.

I am no longer young. I am no longer able to have the stamina I once had. I no longer have the disposition I once had. I no longer have my husband to fill in the weak spots, to take up the slack, to cover my ass.

On top of all the Easter festivities, two new RV's rolled in, and one tent camper who wanted nothing more than to talk for hours on end. The phone rang incessantly, inquiring as to whether I was open today, or would be tomorrow. A couple of well-meaning friends called. It was crazy and crazy-making.

And now, now everyone is gone and the panic has begun. I realize I can't handle this whole scene any more. I can't handle the ranch, the business, the family, the lawyers, the friends or the readying of the ranch for sale. I can't handle missing Trey every moment. I can't handle the thought that I will never see him again in this life. I can't handle the idea of facing the rest of my life without him. I am overburdened and overwrought and I want to disappear.

48

GOING GOING . . .

ONE HECTIC DAY BLEEDS INTO the next with old issues, new issues, and special issues all happening all at once. I have decided to close the ranch to "walk-in" tourists. I have decided to keep the shop open by appointment only. I suppose I can still handle rv's and cabin renters for a while more, but that, too, remains to be seen.

With all the work that appears to be necessary to get this ranch on the market, I don't have time to actually run three or four businesses at the same time and keep what sanity I have left.

As an example of how the simplest thing can drive me to distraction, some friends and I went into town for lunch. Upon my return approximately 3 hours later, I found a note in my door with a five-dollar bill attached. The note said "Thank you for the two items I picked up. I hope $5.00 is sufficient. If not, email me at _____."

Once again, I can't leave for any length of time without someone taking advantage of the situation. I feel like a captive to this ranch. I was furious. And so, I wrote an email to the trespasser stating: "Hello, Ma'am: When I returned home today I got your note and

$5.00. Your note stated that you hoped $5 was sufficient for the items you took. Since I don't know exactly what you took, I have no idea if you paid too much or too little. At this point, that is not what is important to me. What IS important to me is to find out why you thought it would be okay to take anything from someone else's property? If I come to your home, may I take whatever I please and leave you a note and a $5.00 bill?

On your behalf I will say this: at least you left your contact information. Every time I leave the ranch for even a couple of hours (like today), I return to find a note saying someone has felt free to take something. At least you left your contact information, and that is a first. I have always been baffled that anyone would take such liberty on someone else's property.

It is because of practices such as yours, and other similar transgressions, that soon the ranch will be closed to the public for good. I am sorry to belabor the point, especially to someone who was honest enough to leave contact information. But, I am simply stunned by the lack of respect shown to me and the ranch."

Soon the woman, whoever she was, responded by email. She wrote, "I am VERY sorry. I will mail the items back to you when I get back home and you can consider the $5 a small and obviously inadequate payment for your aggravation. I believe your sign leading to your property could be clearer that you are open to visitors only at certain times. I will make sure that the tourist guides and TripAdvisor that I used to plan the trip know that they need to make it clear you are only open limited hours and that people should call ahead to make sure that you are open before arriving (esp. since you are considering closing to the public entirely). I certainly did not mean you any disrespect."

So now I see a perfect example of how people sometimes rationalize their actions, and, when discovered in wrongful behavior, lash out instead of taking personal responsibility. The woman was not sorry, despite her statement of such. When you are sorry about something you have done, the best course is to make a sincere apology. A sincere apology includes a statement defining your offense. A sincere apology asks for forgiveness from the one who has suffered the offense. A sincere apology asks what can be done to rectify the situation.

Her email response only pointed out her own pettiness and attempt to shift the blame for her misbehavior to me. My hours and days of operation are clearly stated on my sign and on my website. That was just another hurtful spear thrown in my direction. After fifteen years of operating the ranch, giving away hundreds of pounds of rocks and fossils to teachers for their classroom use, giving samples away to young customers, taking time to teach how to discover the treasures on the ranch, taking time to go through each person's collection at the end of their excursion and identify what they have collected, taking children on countless (free) tours of the ranch museum, playing games with each child visitor to teach them the joy in finding natural artifacts, her cruel statement is a thinly veiled attempt to discredit me and the ranch.

Such is the stuff of operating a retail business. I'm reading "*The Four Agreements*", and trying mightily not to take anything personally, as the second agreement in the book teaches. It's hard.

49

PUBLIC SHOP, PRIVATE HELL

EVERYTHING BEGAN MOVING AT WARP speed, and suddenly. I had friends/customers ("frustomers?") staying in the rv park, clients staying in the cabins, in short, plenty to do. I could barely keep up. In fact, I really wasn't "keeping up." Many chores had to be left until some undetermined date, and those chores were usually the ones that gave me the most pleasure. Things like a clean house, good food instead of some junk food grabbed out of necessity, a haircut, a hot tub . . . all of those pleasures had to wait for weeks into the future.

One job was to spend an entire day with the ranch appraiser. We drove to places on the ranch I had not been to in years. We found all the boundary fences. We found sign of elk. We jumped at least eight deer napping under some brush. At least this endeavor was out of the ordinary and fun. But since I had still not recovered my energy from the Easter fiasco, the day drained my energy. And when I got home, there were still calls to return, emails to answer, and rv guests to spend time with. It dawned on me that selling the ranch would be adding another full-time job to my already overcrowded schedule. I practically cried when I realized it would be me taking interested buyers all over the ranch. It would be me finding an attorney in Alpine or Midland to draw up contracts. It would be me advertising the ranch for sale. Obviously, something had to go. I had no more time to add more jobs and certainly no more energy. I hastily devised a new plan. It's true what they say: "Necessity is the mother of invention."

I decided that I would only have the shop open for customers who were staying here on the ranch, either in RV sites or in a cabin. I could no longer let people just drive up, pay their day fee, take up hours of my time, and keep me tethered to the shop. Now they would have to actually stay on the ranch. "How had I missed this opportunity before now?" I wondered. This would reduce my work load and possibly increase my income. I could still keep the shop open three days a week for the general public. But the real fun of actually hunting for your own artifacts would be reserved for those who actually wanted to be here for more reasons than just hauling away nature's treasures. This new plan felt workable. It felt like I had just made a huge stride towards restoring some privacy in my life. I put the word out to the general public, and had the website reworked. I felt like this was a good plan for everyone; me and my customers.

Two days later, the rock crowd from the annual rock show began arriving. Generally, folks interested in nature and all the geology of the ranch are really nice people. Generally, they have interesting stories to tell about the other places they've been to hunt rocks, and what they have found once they're there. It becomes a fairly intimate circle of friends, almost friends, friends of friends, and "I've heard about you, friends." But once in a while someone "new" appears. And this was my lucky week.

His name was Samuel and I had received an email from him the previous week saying he wanted to come and camp out during the rock show and hunt agates. I informed him I no longer had camping available, but he could certainly come and hunt. I explained that these three days of the show would be the last three days the ranch was open to the general public for rock hunting. After Saturday, one would have to stay on the ranch to be allowed to roam. He said he would arrive on Thursday.

When the happy day arrived, he stepped out of his jeep and announced that he was Samuel and was here to "hunt malachite."

"Hi, Samuel," I sang out in my friendliest voice, "I remember you from your email. I'm sorry, but malachite is not found here on the ranch, so I'm afraid you'll be disappointed in that department," I added.

"Well, your brochure SAYS you have malachite!" he snarled.

Since I knew I didn't even have a brochure, I felt fairly confident in saying, "Oh, really? Show me the brochure."

He dug around in his jeep and then pulled out a Texas travel book. Quickly scanning the text he said in a lowered tone, "Oh. Not malachite, I'm here to hunt labradorite."

"Well, labradorite I have," I said, again sounding cheerful and ignoring his discordant tone. "Come on in."

I gave him a tour of the shop. I went over the map of the ranch that I give to every customer, and I pointed out the "good" roads and the "bad" roads. He replied that since he had a jeep, "I can go anywhere."

"Well," I laughed, "if you want your nice new jeep to look like my truck, then I guess you can!"

Somehow, I had missed the niggling signs of trouble. My intuition was not alarmed. What I call my "creep radar" had not activated. His initial belligerent attitude had seemed to calm the more we talked about rocks, and by the time he left to go hunting we had covered all the rules of the ranch, and much knowledge of what he might find.

Friends were coming for the weekend, and when they arrived around 4:00, surprisingly, Samuel was with them. They had found him walking up the county lane to the shop, some five miles from where he left his jeep. Eventually, the story came out.

He had gone down one of the "bad" roads (the one I expressly told him not to travel). When he got to the bottom of the moun-tainous road, he decided it was too rough to drive back up. He decided to drive the flat road to the gate of the ranch on the highway. That accomplished with no trouble, he then realized he had forgotten the combination of the gate and had not written it down on his map. His next decision was to walk back to the ranch headquarters, thinking it was only about a mile away. Actually, it was more like five miles. Without water, he began the hike.

Fortunately, one of the sheriff's deputies stopped to question him and had given him a bottle of water. My friends drove him the last mile or so to the headquarters. Now he wanted me to drive him back to the gate where his jeep was parked.

I told him I would, but first to come sit on the patio, cool off and finish his water. My friends, Samuel and I retreated to the shady patio and began discussing his chain of events. "Why did you go down that road when I told you how awful it is?" I asked, sounding incredulous.

"You didn't tell me not to go down that road," he retorted with an annoyed tone.

"Well, yes I did," I reminded him, "I told you it was steep, and at a 45 degree angle, and that your nice new jeep would look like my old truck if you took it down there . . . remember?"

Naively, I was thinking he really didn't remember. Then I saw him glaring at me. And just like that, my "creep radar" started to sound. I don't remember what he said next, but the tone was again snarly.

"I'll take you back to your jeep," I said, "but I'll have to charge you a little extra." He shrugged and waived his hand as if to say, "That's no problem."

About that time, my other friends from the rv park were leaving to go on a picnic with their invited cousins. I thought they were going to the gate where Samuel's jeep was parked, and asked if they could take him with them. They weren't going that way, but offered to change their plans and take him anyway. But first, they had to unload a backseat of picnic supplies so that he would have a place to sit.

It sounded like I was asking far too much of them, but being the wonderful friends, they are, they insisted. And so it was arranged, and Samuel left with them to retrieve his jeep, and then return to pay for the agate he had collected.

Samuel shortly returned and together we went through his collected treasure. Several large stones were incomplete, so I gave them to him. He had a small piece of labradorite that was too small to facet, and I gave him that as well. We went inside and I wrote up his ticket, adding $20.00 for the people who took him to his jeep.

When I handed him the ticket, he exploded.

"This is BULLSHIT!" he screamed.

So startled by this outburst I jumped and, surprised, asked, "What are you talking about?"

Again he yelled, "This is BULLSHIT! I can see adding $10.00, but $20.00?"

"Sir," I began, "Those people used their gas and wear and tear on their vehicle, unloaded supplies so that you would have a place to sit, then took up their time to take you all the way back to your vehicle, and you think $20.00 is exorbitant?"

My mind was twisting a mile a minute and I was incredulous that even after giving him probably $40 worth of material, he would have the gall to scream at me over $20.00.

He never replied to my question. Instead, he leaned over the counter and, looking directly into my eyes, said in a lowered and menacing tone, "I . . . hope . . . you . . . lose . . . everything."

He followed that with, "You're a god-damned bitch."

I don't know what I thought I was going to do, but the look in my eyes as I came around from behind the counter prompted him to quickly throw his money down, turn, and walk rapidly to the door of the shop and down the sidewalk. For the first time I knew what it meant: "HELL hath no fury like a woman scorned!"

"Seriously, Sir?" I asked, following him down the sidewalk, "You're seriously going to treat a woman like you just did over $20.00? Really, sir? Really? What a gentleman!" I was like a dog with a bone, nipping at his heels, being polite, but not letting up.

He muttered under his breath all the way to his vehicle, threw his collection into the jeep, got himself in, and drove away in a hurry, sending gravel and rocks flying all over the parking lot.

I stood there, silently amazed. I realized at that instant that I had unwittingly made a correct and much needed choice. My decision to close the ranch to the general public was, indeed, the right thing to do. I had been so long out of "civilization" I had no idea that people now react with such rudeness and downright malice. Fortunately, my friends were still sitting on the patio, unaware of what had just transpired. But what if I had been alone, as I usually am? What if I had driven him by myself to his vehicle? What might he have done on that stretch of lonesome road?

At that moment I felt very alone, and I realized that all of my "bravery" of living in the middle of nowhere, running a public business where anyone can walk in at any time, was nothing more

123

than asking for trouble. I realized that, while I may be good at selling ecotourism, my world was not the same as it was only a year ago. I no longer have any "back-up." It is still, after all, a man's world. And my man is gone.

50

GUNS AND JESUS

TWO DAYS LATER I WENT to a class that begins the process of obtaining a concealed carry license, or, CCL. In Texas, you can always carry a concealed handgun in your car when you are on a public road, and you can certainly have one, or in my case, some, in your own home. But actually, having the license to carry a concealed handgun informs your psyche that you are prepared. Sure, in some circles it's not politically correct to have any kind of gun, let alone a handgun. But this is Texas. And I am a Texan. And I have tarried too long on this isolated road without some protection.

And so I went to the class. It was informative. It was fun. And then we went to the shooting range. As it turns out, I'm a damn good shot. Out of a possible score of 250, I got 248. The target is a large outline of the human body. All of the nice little bullet holes I made were inside the main torso. I brought it home for a souvenir. Now I carry a .380 semi-auto on my person, a .22 mag revolver in my car, and have two shotguns and a 9mm semi-auto rifle next to my bed. As the old joke goes, "What are you afraid of?" Answer: "Not a damn thing."

And then a new concern arose, but still within my newly adopted "protection plan." I realized that I was missing more than just my husband. I was missing worshiping something bigger than myself. I was missing fellowship with other spiritual people. I was missing some kind of feeling of comfort on a deeper, soul level. I decided to start visiting the churches in my small town to see where I might "fit."

The first church was very formal. The music was not anything I recognized from my days of growing up in the Baptist and Methodist churches. It was a "busy" church, with all kinds of dinners, classes, and projects to get involved in. Some of my friends were members, but they rarely went. Both Sundays I sat alone in a pew that was empty. I was uncomfortable.

The next church I visited was loud, informal, and had a band. I knew a few people there, but not well. The building was a large metal barn-type building. The huge metal rolling doors opened on two sides, and the beauty of God's West Texas was right there to look at. The breeze would blow softly across the congregation, easing your mind and your spirit. The people were up-beat and laid back. The dress was jeans, shorts, cowboy hats, boots, sandals . . . in short, my kind of place.

I had met the preacher once, just a couple of months after Trey died. He was, in fact, a foreman on a neighboring ranch. He and his beautiful wife were welcoming and kind, but not "pushy." Again, I sat alone in the row of seats I chose.

I attended several times, and then invited two of my best friends to go one Sunday. They loved it, too. It feels comfortable. It feels like Texas. Which, as everyone knows, is the closest place to heaven this side of the River Styx.

51

IS IT THE END?

SOMETHING HAS CHANGED. SOMETHING ESSENTIAL to my very core is changing, morphing, into something else. Yes, I'm still consumed at times by the waves of loneliness and missing Trey. Yes, sometimes I feel anger that I can't control because Trey and I didn't have more time together. Yes, sadness weeps out of my very pores when I pass certain spots on the ranch, hear "our" song, or face yet another challenge that I feel unprepared for doing alone. What has changed is that I don't feel those feelings *all the time*. They come . . . they go. Yes, sometimes they come and stay longer and at those times I hide myself away not answering telephones or even opening my business. But they do go.

And then a bit of comfort from the storm appears in some small form and for a few . . . hours? Days? I can breathe again. Sometimes, when I'm having a laugh with a few friends, or a hilarious joke comes through email, I actually forget that I'm forging a new life and trying to be brave enough to see it through. It's like, *forgetting to remember.*

I'm somewhat amazed that fifteen months have passed since

Trey's death. With each new passing challenge, accomplishment, endeavor, I used to try to figure out what Trey would have wanted, or would have done if he were here. Sometimes the unknowingness of what he would have done brought absolute despair. But now, more often than not, I just barge ahead, pretending (if nothing else) that I know what I'm doing.

To try and bolster my self-confidence, I recount my accomplishments to myself. I've taken care of the cows and horses and then completed their sale. I leased the pastures. I maintained the deer lease. I had the water leak at the cabins repaired. I had the east road maintained. I've completely re-done the water system, twice. I've worked with the appraiser until the completion of the appraisal instrument. I've shown the ranch to a prospective buyer, (not so easy when you're the one opening all the gates). I've met and contracted with a surveyor. I've worked out an agreement with my brother-in-law. I've sold the jeep and the cattle trailer. I've had new lines run to the 1,000 gallon propane tank. I've had locks put on all the doors. I've had the roof repaired. I've had the old storage building that was blown to pieces in a small tornado torn down and removed. I've emptied the warehouse of all old tools and collected junk, and had two garage sales to try and get rid of it.

Just making the list makes me tired. To see all of what has transpired actually written down on paper, and to know that it was all done *while I was still running the shop, the rv park and the cabins*, is amazing. It is even more amazing to know that I did this while I was trying to grieve. Maybe that's the *way* I grieve, by staying so busy I can't think. I can't remember. I can't dwell.

But now this new change brings its own burdens. I sometimes feel I'm losing even more of Trey, if that's possible. Sometimes, I'm terrified that the hole he left in my life will remain open, gaping, and unfilled forever. Sometimes I'm afraid that it won't; that it will somehow glaze over with time and distance and a healing scar, and I will be left with nothing.

This life and death thing is heavy and deep and complicated, with new facets appearing at every milestone.

52

ONE MORE STEP

THE APPRAISAL ON THE RANCH is finally done. I have a neat little folder that holds all the facts and figures of the "value" of the ranch. I have told no one. I have spent five days just thinking it over, going over in my mind the ins and outs of what this means. My body has cooperated by getting sick, enabling me to spend most of any idle time I have each day to sit, and think.

I must find an attorney. There are contracts to write and people to notify. The buyers who contacted me last fall should know that bid packages will be ready soon. I need to talk with my brother-in-law and together set our asking price for the ranch. All of this comes on Memorial Day weekend when, by fate or luck, offices that I need to contact are closed. Tuesday will be the day I find an attorney. Wednesday, I have a couple coming for the small cabin. Friday and Saturday, I have the garage sale of all the tools and "stuff" left over from the sale of last November. Hopefully this time I can make a little money, as I will hold it in town and not on the ranch. I just paid the appraiser $2800 and need to pay the last mortgage note of $4000. Then of course, the attorney will have to be paid. I am beginning to feel a little "squeezed" for cash. I'm starting to feel anxious. It's the craziest thing. Just when my life appears to be moving forward, the anxiety sets in. I don't want to be in a hurry to sell the ranch. In fact, I don't care whether it sells at all. Is that attitude really how I feel, or is it the fear of moving on?

It's probably the fear of moving on. I try to prop myself up again. I congratulate myself that the appraisal value is more or less what I had said it would be before the appraiser was even contracted. I wonder whether I should really try to get an attorney to do sealed bids, or whether, in the long run, a realtor would be the easiest, and cheapest, way to go. After all, do I really want to spend my last summer on the ranch dealing with buyers, taking them all over the ranch, "talking shop?" No. I don't. Even though I feel like I could stay here forever, there is a clock ticking, and that clock is maintenance. All last year I worked on the projects I had the knowledge to complete. I don't have the knowledge or the where-with-all to tackle the many jobs of keeping the ranch maintained. Knowing what is ahead for the major maintenance of the ranch gives me a timeline of about a year.

And so I got referrals from anyone who would know, for the best title company in the area. I made an appointment with them. I was given the most straight-forward and pertinent advice I'd ever received. The agent gave me a quick run-through of just how a real estate sale progresses and what I would need to be aware of at every turn. We covered what the title company does, what the appraisal is, what the survey is and when it is ordered, who orders it, and who pays for it. This lady knew her business and was eager to share it with me. I learned the value of doing business with professionals. If I didn't know the answers, at least I knew where to ask the questions.

53

A MOMENTARY LAPSE

THE PHONE RINGS AND IT is a dear friend. We catch up on all the news of our lives and then move on to the progress on the sale of the ranch. I tell her I've got the appraisal done and, while I'm not giving out the bottom-line figure to anyone, I can say that I am quite happy with it. Her tone immediately changes.

"What do you mean you're not going to give out the figure?" she questions.

"Well, that's private, business information and I just don't want it floating around," I respond in my most competent voice.

We begin to discuss the other information on the ranch. She tells me my information is wrong. I MUST get a survey done and done NOW. If there are only three surveyors in the local area I should go to Austin and get someone to come out.

"And should I just have them send the $50,000.00 bill to you?" I inquire. "Of course I'm not getting a surveyor all the way from Austin! Don't be ridiculous!" I add.

"Well there are always costs associated with selling your property and you'll just have to assume those costs," she retorted with condescension dripping out of her voice.

The conversation devolved from there. In her opinion I was wrong about the estimated value of the ranch I had mentioned, wrong about the information from the "bogus" title company, wrong about saying I was in no hurry to sell the ranch. In short, I was just wrong, incompetent to handle such a huge business situation, and incapable of leading my life without, apparently, her supervision.

Stunned, I asked her to take a breath and listen. She wouldn't, but continued her denigrating rant without pause. Finally I said, "You have not said one positive word since this conversation started. Everything you have said is completely negative. I can't listen to this anymore. I'm sorry, but I have to go now."

She responded by saying she "loved me" and didn't want me to make any huge mistakes. Remembering what the Bible says love is (Cor.), I responded that it just didn't feel like love, it felt like badgering. On that note we said our good-byes and hung up.

I didn't want to take it personally. I wanted to tell myself that she was just having a bad day. I wanted to think I could figure out what her hidden agenda was. None of that worked. I ended up feeling incompetent, afraid and betrayed. The feeling lasted for two days. After all the angst and emotional upheaval, I finally let it go. Life is too fast and too crowded to indulge in such useless emotion that only serves to eat up my time. When you truly let go of such a burden, the veil of life changes immediately. The clouds clear, you effortlessly move on. The new feeling somehow transfuses the entire fabric of reality, and reaches out to everyone involved. The next day she called.

We chatted and laughed our way through the call, being careful not to touch the sore spots. I relearned a valuable lesson. It's not always about ME. Sometimes it's about THEM.

54

JUNE 5

EXACTLY FIFTEEN MONTHS SINCE TREY died. The count goes on, and, I suppose, it never stops. There will always be an anniversary date. There will always be a sense of great loss. There will always be those who tell you to "get over it." There will always be those who will say, "You're a widow now. Act like it." I don't know how I made it to the last quarter of my life without knowing that people will always judge you, no matter what course of action you may choose. Evidently I have been a real Pollyanna throughout my life. But I am tougher now, just when I understand enough to want to consciously be softer. I am more tired now, just when I consciously begin to notice fresh, new creative ideas. What timing I have!

55

SUMMER, AGAIN

TRADITIONAL SUMMER RAINS HAVE BEGUN, seeming to wash away some of the horror of last year. This time *last* year I was so veiled in grief I saw nothing through the wafting smoke lingering from the awful fires that engulfed most of the county. This time *last* year I prayed for dawn because the nights held such sad memories and terrifying thoughts of the present. This time *last* year I had cows to feed, no water, almost unbearable heat, and a mind full of worries that acted like a stone fence holding "normal" life at bay. *This* year something has changed. And it has caught me unawares.

Childhood friends come to spend a few days with me. We have such fun remembering our girlhoods, laughing at ourselves, and pondering completely non-weighty fancies. Having friends to go out to eat with is fun again. Coming home to a not-empty house is fun again. Having friends to share the ranch with is fun again. The sickening scab of loneliness and sorrow is beginning to dissolve. I allow myself a beginning feeling of hope. Maybe I'll live after all.

56

THE BEGINNING OF THE END

I HAD VAGUELY KNOWN HIM for almost a year. We were introduced at an Easter dinner the previous year and had seen each other at several functions over the intervening months. But for all that time, being wrapped in the dense fog of painful grief, he was just another face, appearing from time to time in the focus of my random consciousness. And then an accidental meeting at a store parking lot on just the perfect day, at just the perfect time, had led him to call me and arrange a brief visit over drinks. While the invitation hung on the telephone line I remembered how he had looked that day, with the late afternoon sun backlighting his face and curly silver hair gleaming like a halo. "Wow, you look positively *angelic*," I had said without thinking and out of complete surprise at the visual effects. He looked bemused.

We had drinks. We had long conversations on topics other than death. He didn't once ask, "How are you doing?" He was funny, with a tart, acerbic sense of humor. He was smart, and I didn't have to explain anything I said, or anything I left unsaid. I liked him. And, as our visits continued, I decided I liked him a lot.

This first tentative foray back into the land of the living was like walking back into time. Remembering how it felt to be fourteen and have new feelings, and fearsome desires, and emotions that swung, pendulum-like, through all the gamuts of human interaction and yet not knowing *how* to feel, *what* to fear or what the rules were, was suddenly my experience . . . again. It was exhausting, this re-awakening, and left no time for all the other things that had become my routine since Trey's death. Now there was no time to sit and ponder what death felt like, no time to try and communicate with the dearly, and now clearly, departed, no time for freakish storms of remorse and guilt and tears.

I wanted to slink back into the safety of grief. I wanted to scream. I wanted to cry. I wanted to hold on. I wanted to let go. I wanted to be anywhere but caught in this never-ending dichotomy.

In my mind I compared it to being a recent amputee. The anesthesia mercifully takes you down, down into complete abyss. When you wake, there is a tingling where the limb used to be, a barely felt remembrance of something that was there, and then it wasn't. This "getting back into life" was like that. I *almost* felt the remembrance of a lovers' kiss, the sudden welling of lost desire. Almost . . . and then fear set in and I was back to being fourteen.

I didn't know how to respond. I was afraid of appearing silly. I was afraid of being taken advantage of. I was afraid I didn't know the new rules of relationship. I was afraid it was too soon. I was afraid it was too late.

One day a girlfriend asked if I was seeing anyone yet. "No," I lied, hoping the reply was firm enough for the conversation to take a different turn. I was never a good liar.

"Why not?" my friend asked, missing the subtlety of my short answer.

The question made me hesitate and actually think about it.

While not ready to admit it, I knew I was tired to death of the loneliness of widowhood. But I also knew I was even more scared of starting life over. I decided to put the truth in a frame different from both of those meanderings. "Well, Trey actually *adored* me. I mean, he put me on a pedestal and no matter what I said or did, he kept me there. No one has ever treated me the way Trey did. I guess I got used to it."

"Adoration is a pretty high bar to set," my friend went on. "I suggest you lower your expectations!" We both had a good laugh and the conversation went on to other topics.

One early summer evening I invited my new friend to go with me to a gathering deep in the heart of the desert. It was a memorial for my friend, Evelyn, to be held in the desert, on the outreaches of her ranch. Having died the previous Christmas, her children and grandchildren were saying a final good-bye.

I wanted my new friend to see my beautiful desert for the first time with me. I wanted to share with him a part of my life that had helped to mold me into the person I was now. I wanted him to see a glimpse of who I had been before widowhood. I wanted to remember myself.

I was hesitant to call and ask him to go to the gathering with me. The last time I "dated" had been some twenty years ago. What was the protocol for invitations these days? Was I being too "forward?" Was I letting myself in for some major rejection? What would he think? Was he just being kind to a woman who was clumsily trying to find her way back into life? As I continued the spiraling debate with myself, the phone rang. It was him.

"What are you doing?" he asked point blank.

"Well, I'm watching a movie and trying to decide what to do," I responded, mesmerized by the idea that he would call at such a coincidental time, and ask such a direct question.

"What movie are you watching?" he wanted to know.

Laughing out loud I admitted, "He's Just Not That Into You."

"And what are you trying to decide?" He was relentless.

"Well if you really want to know, I'm trying to decide whether or not to invite you to a funeral. Well, not exactly a funeral, it's a celebration of life . . . a memorial for a long-time friend of mine. Funerals, memorials, departed souls, I'm just a barrel of fun, aren't I?" I answered, suddenly astounded that I had invited him, and now feeling shy. I continued trying to explain myself but he interrupted and blurted out, "Yes. I want to go. I want to go with you."

It was a short 70 mile drive to the site, and a good bottle of Merlot turned the car into a slow, albeit illegal, ride. I felt comfortable, encased in the insulated car, air conditioner providing a cool breeze, a beautiful summer night, good company. Even though we drove slowly on the country road we arrived with a lot of conversation still left unsaid. It was going to be a full moon night, and I knew it would be the perfect way to say good-bye to Evelyn, and possibly even say good-by to some of the sadness of Trey's death. After all, this west Teas desert held so much of my life, so many memories, so many secrets.

The desert floor was decorated with white luminarias, already lighted even before sunset. The bare hills surrounded us and as I moved among all the old friends from a different chapter of my life, the orange and gold and pink tones of twilight began to light the hills with a glow that seemingly came from within them. Like embers, the luminescent light penetrated the air. At the same time, a full moon rose over the back of the hills, casting its silver glow like a patina onto everything. It took my breath away. I was seized with gratitude that suddenly I was able to again appreciate magnificent beauty, even in the stark midst of the nightmare that life can sometimes be. Like a newborn taking her first sharp gulp of air, I realized I had taken a fork in the road of my despair. I could feel again. I could laugh again. I was on the mend.

57

I WISH I HAD KNOWN

I WISH I HAD KNOWN that when your spouse dies, everything else can wait. The family can wait, the business can wait, the chores can wait, eating can wait, corresponding can wait, plans can wait. The initial days and weeks after spousal death will later seem like a blur, and you won't remember what you did or what you said anyway.

I wish I had known that my spouse's credit cards would be canceled if my name was not also on the account.

I wish I had known that when your spouse dies, your own family and your spouse's family will undoubtedly try to "help." The "help" may be non-existent and the stress will be unbearable. Ask them to come later.

I wish I had known that sometimes friends and family members will take items your spouse loved. They will rationalize this theft by way of thinking they just want one little remembrance of the departed. They will rationalize that you are too overwrought to bother asking for the item, and certainly wouldn't mind them having it. "Besides," they will continue, "she wouldn't want it anyway and won't even notice that it's gone." They are, of course, wrong about this, and when you come to your senses you will be surprised to see items missing from their usual habitats. You will spend too much time looking for these items. You will think yourself forgetful at best, and crazy at worst. Eventually, probably months or years later, when you have looked everywhere there is to look, you will realize the truth.

I wish I had known to ask one or two of my most trusted friends to take telephone calls and reply to emails. The constant retelling of the events leading up to the death are heartbreaking to say the least. You will quickly become drained of any energy you thought you had.

I wish I had known that the people who really care about you will, by themselves, find a way to be of service to you. They will be able to see what is needed and take care of it, without bothering you with details. They will be your biggest blessing.

I wish I had known that rest is the best medicine.

I wish I had known that my pets were grieving, too.

I wish I had known how to deal with the pain of not being able to say "goodbye."

I wish I had known that it is okay to cry in front of other people. At such a time, it is even okay to "ugly cry" in front of other people.

I wish I had known, really known, that a time would come when the grief would not be unbearable, but transformed into something else. Transformed into something undefinable for anyone save yourself. Something easier to live with. Something your heart remembers.

ABOUT JAYSON WOODWARD

Author photo by Gina Ciaccio Photography

Learning to navigate her way through a dangerous and disintegrating family, Jayson Woodward has been writing and counseling in one form or another her entire life. Reaching adulthood, she went on to earn a B.S. Degree in Education and Writing, and then a M.Ed. degree in counseling.

She became a certified teacher and taught writing for ten years. She counseled young clients in a school setting over issues which she, herself,was all too acquainted.

"I believe books and writings of any kind that reach people can positively impact their lives," has been a mantra throughout her life. In *The Heart Remembers*, her numerous short stories and songs, all reflect the power of people, especially women, to overcome adversity with mercy and forgiveness.

In *Borderline*, her second book, she focused her narrative to inspire readers to overcome challenges associated with victimhood, while teaching basic information in defending against predation.

A well-seasoned traveler, Ms. Woodward has lived near many borders: the southwestern border of the United States, Belize, Guatemala, Costa Rica and Peru. Her travels have served to broaden her interests in geology, gemstones and jewelry making and to enrich her understanding of life through cultures different from her own.

As a single mother to a son, she learned that wit and humor can go a long way to survival of almost anything. In fact, while trying to grow up in her birth family, comedy became one of her strongest coping skills. And so throughout her writings, the reader will sometimes come across humorous writings in the most solemn places. "Humor diffuses stress, and life is all about dis-tress and eu-stress. Laugh a little."

Jayson lives in the southwest and continues to write.

Jayson is available to speak to groups and events about a range of topics associated with *surviving and thriving*, and *growth through grief*.

Follow Jayson
www.jaysonwoodward.com
www.facebook.com/jaysonwoodward
www.twitter.com/jaysonwoodward

Made in the USA
Lexington, KY
24 October 2019